Critical Acts

CRITICAL ACTS

Latin American Women
and Cultural Criticism

Elizabeth A. Marchant

University Press of Florida
Gainesville · Tallahassee · Tampa · Boca Raton
Pensacola · Orlando · Miami · Jacksonville

04 03 02 01 00 99 6 5 4 3 2 1

LIBRARY OF CONGRESS CATALOGING-IN-PUBLICATION DATA
Marchant, Elizabeth A. 1962–
Critical acts : Latin American women and cultural criticism / Elizabeth A. Marchant.
p. cm.
Includes bibliographical references and index.
ISBN 0-8130-1683-5 (alk. paper)
1. Criticism—Latin America. 2. Women critics—Latin America. 3. Latin American
literature—History and criticism. 4. Literature and society—Latin America. 5. Pereira,
Lúcia Miguel, 1901–1959. 6. Ocampo, Victoria, 1890–1979. 7. Mistral, Gabriela, 1889–
1957. I. Title.
PN99.L29M34   1999
860.9'9287—dc21   98-47241

The University Press of Florida is the scholarly publishing agency for the State University
System of Florida, comprised of Florida A & M University, Florida Atlantic University,
Florida International University, Florida State University, University of Central Florida,
University of Florida, University of North Florida, University of South Florida, and
University of West Florida.

University Press of Florida
15 Northwest 15th Street
Gainesville, FL 32611–2079
http://www.upf.com

To Rafa, for his courage.

CONTENTS

Preface   ix

1. The Bearded Academy   1

2. Lúcia Miguel Pereira and the Era(c)ing of
   Brazilian National Literature   18

3. From Consumption to Production: Victoria Ocampo
   as Cultural Critic   46

4. Nation and Motherhood in Gabriela Mistral   80

Afterword   107

Notes   109

Works Cited   131

Index   139

PREFACE

Interest in Latin American women's writing has grown steadily over the past three decades. With the resulting expansion of the corpus of texts written by women, new possibilities for understanding their position within Latin American societies emerge. As part of an ongoing effort to reconsider the scene of writing for Latin American women, *Critical Acts* examines the literary and cultural criticism produced by Lúcia Miguel Pereira (Brazil), Victoria Ocampo (Argentina), and Gabriela Mistral (Chile) during the first half of the twentieth century. Focusing on the broad national and historical contexts in which these authors wrote, this book pays particular attention to the critical strategies and generic disruptions they employed in their writings. It recuperates and analyzes their cultural work, highlighting the historical importance of writing by women in Latin America. Most specifically, *Critical Acts* shows how, given the predominant tendency to view women as writers of the personal, they nonetheless gave voice to their views on culture, race, gender, and national identity.

Critical Acts will appeal to readers interested in women's studies, in Latin American studies, and in twentieth-century Brazilian and Spanish American literature. More generally, anyone interested in theories of identity and location, especially with regard to gender, will find this study particularly useful.

This project was supported financially by research grants from the University of California. I am grateful for the encouragement and advice of Dale Bauer, Silvia Bermúdez, Ernesto Chávez, John Coleman, Ana Paula Ferreira, John Foran, Avery Gordon, Heloísa Buarque de Hollanda, Gordon Hutner, Randal Johnson, Jane Kamenksy, Gwen Kirkpatrick, Jim Mandrell, Francine Masiello, Chris Newfield, Marta Peixoto, Emma Pérez, Susan C. Quinlan, Chela Sandoval, and Sylvia Wynter. Librarians Adán Griego and Nerea Llamas provided warm friendship and crucial bibliographic support as did my research assistant, Marcia Rodríguez. I offer my special thanks to Sylvia Molloy, whose input was instrumental to the original development of this project. Charles Cutler, my first and most enduring mentor, continues to be an inspiration. Thanks, too, to the anonymous readers for the University Press of Florida who offered such useful and intelligent suggestions.

For their abiding interest and emotional (and sometimes technical) support, I thank my family—Ted, Wilma, Judy, Jim, Jess, and Jeannette Marchant, Kin Seto, Teresa Pérez, Rafael Pérez Sandoval, and Estela and Scott Narrie.

Finally, my greatest thanks to my partner, my heart, Rafael Pérez-Torres, for his tireless support but mostly for staying on *this* plane of existence.

1

The Bearded Academy

The three women focused upon here, acting as agents in history, work against the impoverished roles scripted for them as *prote(c)toras* of the private. Three Latin American women—Lúcia Miguel Pereira, Victoria Ocampo, and Gabriela Mistral—chose the act of writing as a way to intervene in the public realm of literary criticism being developed in the first half of the twentieth century. Their work provides a body of critical writing—at times resistant, at others acquiescent—that not only comments upon the development of literary production but also reveals the difficulties women encounter in claiming a public voice in Latin America. The discursive strategies their works employ are multiple and range from the extension of the personal beyond its customary gendered limits to careful mimicry of nationalist discourses on culture to the formation of a women's nationalist project distinct from (at times critical of) traditional nationalism. By spotlighting their work, this book examines both the possibilities of women's engagement with critical discourse and the status of woman as a historical subject in Latin America. It thus scrutinizes the ways in which cultural concerns are articulated within a highly gendered Latin American context.

The ideas presented in the following chapters arise from an initial observation about Brazilian literary history. In studies of nineteenth- and early-twentieth-century Brazilian literature, citations of the literary critical work of Lúcia Miguel Pereira (1901–1959) appear with considerable frequency. A novelist, Miguel Pereira was the only recognized female literary critic of her time in Brazil. As a woman, what is it about her writing that allows her to successfully claim authority and make critical judgments about literature? Moreover, at what cost was she able to adopt a critical position normally available only to men? An examination of her writings reveals a sharp contrast between the concerns voiced in her literary criticism and the themes developed in her novels. In the critical writing, virtually no women writers appear. These writings do, however, include biographies of the founding fathers of Brazilian national literature. By contrast, Miguel Pereira's four novels center exclusively and extensively on women's experiences within familial and social contexts. Chapter two examines this split, placing Miguel Pereira's work within the contexts of Brazilian literary and social history.

From Miguel Pereira, I turn to two other women who attempted to make their voices heard in discussions of literature and culture at roughly the same time. Paying particular attention to the differences between what are customarily seen as their critical writings and their creative writings, I find that this relationship is not the same from one writer to the next. Victoria Ocampo's approach to writing about literature could not be more different from Miguel Pereira's. Ocampo, for example, makes no clear distinction between creative and critical writing. In her *Testimonios,* she carries on conversations with authors, with books, with herself, and with her past. Not surprisingly, her writing is often dismissed as overly personal, and she is not usually taken seriously as a creator of cultural knowledge. While relatively little is known or written about the life of Lúcia Miguel Pereira, when studying Ocampo it is impossible to avoid what others write about her personal history, her personality, and her body. These texts far outnumber those examining Ocampo's actual writing. Miguel Pereira removes herself and virtually all other women writers from her critical texts and is granted the status of a literary critic. By virtue of her personal approach to literature, Ocampo decidedly is not. Chapter three investigates the often negative views of Ocampo and her work and the ways in which she nonetheless produces cultural knowledge.

Like Miguel Pereira, Gabriela Mistral is granted some literary authority. When Pedro Henríquez Ureña addresses the changed social position of the men of letters in Latin American literature from 1890 to 1920 in *Literary Currents in Hispanic America,* Mistral and three other women are grouped with them:

> The men of letters—literature not being really a profession, but an avocation—became journalists or teachers or both. Many still went to the universities to study law, but few practiced it. Some obtained diplomatic or consular posts; the custom is maintained to this day, and it includes women now, such as the Chileans Gabriela Mistral and Marta Brunet, the Cuban Flora Días Parrado, and the Colombian Laura Victoria. (161)

So Mistral is placed within the tradition of men of letters that, for Henríquez Ureña, includes several women. Yet because of the ways in which the category of *hombre de letras* is constructed, her active presence as pedagogue and diplomat cannot be recognized as feminine. There is no such thing as a "mujer de letras." Chapter four interrogates Mistral's designation as "spiritual mother" of Latin America. The facts about her life seem to contradict both this designation of her person as well as the roles she prescribes for other Latin American women.

A brief account of the educational status of women in Latin America in the early twentieth century will help to contextualize our understanding of the role these three women played. Latin American societies undertook widespread educational reform in the latter half of the nineteenth century. For the first time in the region's history, some public education was made available to children of both sexes. The government of Benito Juárez legislated public secondary schools for girls in Mexico in the 1860s, and Domingo F. Sarmiento established public schools in Argentina during the years of his presidency in the 1860s and 1870s. In Brazil, Nísia Floresta founded a school for girls in 1838 and in 1853 published sixty-two essays on the education of women under the title *Opúsculo humanitário*.[1] Still, access to education remained extremely limited for most of the century—little or no formal education was offered to lower-class children of either sex. Upper-class women continued to be tutored in the seclusion of their homes or cloistered away in convent schools as they had been during the colonial period, and all women were barred entirely from the universities. As the middle sectors of some Latin American societies grew, however, the impetus for educational reform gained strength. The reformers tended to be women living in urban areas with close family ties to men working in the law, medicine, the judiciary, and academia. "Their appearance in Buenos Aires, Santiago, Rio de Janeiro, and Mexico in the 1860s and 1870s is directly proportionate to the degree of political stability and economic expansion attained by these societies by the late nineteenth century" (F. Miller *Latin* 44).

Educational reform eventually became widespread with the introduction of normal schools in Chile, Uruguay, Brazil, Mexico, and Argentina. Based on a North American model and centered on normal schools, the reforms enacted by Sarmiento in Argentina included public schooling from kindergarten to secondary school. Designed to educate young students with the skills to become schoolteachers, normal schools provided Latin American women's first opportunity to study beyond the primary level, though they were initially dominated by male students (47). The increased access to education for women did have its limits: normal-school preparation was considered inferior to other secondary schooling, and they were still barred from the universities. And while teaching represented a legitimate career for newly educated women, it could be also defined and circumscribed as an extension of the traditional nurturing role of the mother.[2] As Beatriz Sarlo suggests, in the role of teachers, women did not necessarily present a threat to masculine hegemony over nation and culture as they most often re-produced national ideology ("Women" 234). From this point of view, they could be understood as transmitters rather than creators of knowledge. Despite these limitations, teaching must have encouraged some women to aspire to move into other professions, applying their skills in new areas. A handful of Latin American women did receive university degrees in medicine, dentistry, and law in the 1880s and 1890s (F. Miller *Latin* 49).

Expanded educational opportunities significantly increased the number of literate women and men across Latin America by the turn of the century. Greater readership was accompanied by the growth of print culture. Recent research on the history of women's periodicals reveals that women have been active in publishing in Latin America since the eighteenth century.[3] Evidence gathered from the period between 1722 and 1988 reveals that 377 periodicals written by or for women were published, with Argentina (73), Mexico (55), and Brazil (40) registering the highest totals (Seminar on Women and Culture 184). By 1920, women were involved in the publication of periodicals throughout Latin America. Their activities in publishing had intensified, and they were contributing to journals edited by men and to mainstream newspapers. Because of the international circulation of many publications, journalism played a significant role in unifying geographically distant areas of Latin America. For intellectuals of both sexes, the expansion of print culture provided a new means of economic support.

Given that their activity has received so little attention to date, it has been suggested that the study of women's participation in publishing will entail a rewriting of the history of Latin American culture: "The existence of this women's print network challenges assumptions about the supposed isolation, parochialism, and triviality of women's culture in the nineteenth century" (Seminar 175). The essay was often the form of choice for women publishing in the nineteenth century. Despite the fact that much of this print material has been lost, scholars have begun to recover and analyze these texts. We now know that Latin American women essayists participated in broad networks of writers and that they often focused their concerns on women's participation in society, arguing for educational reform and protection under the law. Francine Masiello has found that in mid-nineteenth-century Argentina, for example, journalistic production by women focused on three areas of discussion: "the home as a safe haven from tyranny and the importance of family obligations; the body as a debatable site for meaning in the public sphere; and the insistence on women's right to receive education and participate in creative activities" ("Between" 529). Actively engaging in debates on the public life of women in society, women writers throughout Latin America worked in the intersection between the literary and social. Lourdes Rojas and Nancy Saporta Sternbach describe the process by which their work was often disseminated:

> A typical trajectory would be as follows: a luminary figure such as Clorinda Matto de Turner or Alfonsina Storni would be invited to give a talk at the Ateneo de Buenos Aires, for example. After declaring herself unworthy of the praise she had just received, a tactic employed to mitigate her radical message, she would then go on to deliver an important speech on women's rights. That speech, in turn, would be printed as a pamphlet and sold for twenty centavos. Many years later, this same speech might be printed as a book. (177–178)

In the cases of the three authors studied herein, recent research by Masiello, Rojas and Saporta Sternbach, and others provides a backdrop that helps highlight the significance of their writings. Thanks to these new developments, it is now more difficult to claim that intellectuals like Ocampo, Miguel Pereira, and Mistral were exceptions or that they worked in isolation. Their own writings attest to connections with other women thinkers and even between them—Victoria Ocampo writes about Gabriela Mistral and vice versa. An examination of women's participation in print culture takes on another dimension when we consider their activity within the context of nation building. Women writers were forming connections and contestations in print during the same period in which Latin American *hombres de letras* were forcefully enacting definitions of national identity through literary genealogies. This simultaneous activity makes studying the approaches to literature and culture voiced by writers like Ocampo, Miguel Pereira, and Mistral all the more compelling.

If, as Sylvia Molloy suggests, "any consideration of women writers in Latin America must take into account that the very term *woman writer* refers to an unstable reality, one that, even now, is not accepted without qualifications" (Molloy "Introduction" 108), what are the ramifications of this instability for those Latin American women writers who dare to intervene in the play of culture? We might want to think beyond what the phrase "woman writer" signifies: the word "woman" itself has proven a complex sign. Judith Butler argues that the definition of the term "woman" is unstable: "If one 'is' a woman, that is surely not all one is; the term fails to be exhaustive, not because a pregendered 'person' transcends the specific paraphernalia of its gender, but because gender is not always constituted coherently or consistently in different historical contexts, and because gender intersects with racial, class, ethnic, sexual, and regional modalities of discursively constituted identities" (3). The term "woman," like the term "writer," is always culturally produced and embedded in a social matrix. In Latin America of the early twentieth century, for example, the character of "woman" emerges from the vexed intersection of sexuality, class, and race and national identity. Generalizing about relations of power based on gender proves difficult because of the complicated interplay between gender and these other axes of power relations. In other words, the construction of gender is culturally and historically specific.

Insofar as the instability to which Molloy refers is a product of discrimination against them simply because they are women, one can justify examination of women writers as a group. Such a grouping does not necessarily suggest an essential role for women. If anything, there are striking differences among the approaches to culture taken by the writers studied here. The works of Lúcia Miguel Pereira, Victoria Ocampo, and Gabriela Mistral emerge from the specific cultural contexts of early-twentieth-century Brazil, Argentina, and Mexico and Chile.[4] Each of these women adopts a different strategy for inserting herself into the scenarios that represent nascent nations in literature and the arts.

This book scrutinizes how three women critics attempt to define and control the social circulation of knowledge within specific cultural contexts. Since culture involves, in part, the struggle to determine meaning, then controlling and making meaning out of cultural products is an exercise of power. Drawing on the work of Raymond Williams, John Fiske describes culture as having "both sense-making and power-bearing functions. Its sense-making function contains concerns such as those of knowledge, discourse, representation, and practice; within its power-bearing functions are those of power, control, discipline, struggle, resistance, and evasion" (13–14). Definitions of these concepts emerge and change with their situation. This book seeks to answer the following questions: What definitions do these terms take on in the contexts of cultural production in the first half of the twentieth century in Latin America? And how do they intersect with the shifting image of the woman writer?

The position of the writer in Latin America raises issues of power for women that are not present in the same form for their counterparts in the United States or Europe. For this reason, feminist literary theory formulated in the "First World" may not always enhance our understanding of feminism in "Third World" spaces as critics such as Chandra Mohanty, Chela Sandoval, and Audre Lorde have indicated. In "Beyond Ethnocentrism: Gender, Power, and the Third-World Intelligentsia," Jean Franco accounts for what she refers to as the "crucial and constitutive" activity of the literary intelligentsia in Latin America: "Because it was blocked from making contributions to the development of scientific thought, the intelligentsia was forced into the one area that did not require professional training and the institutionalization of knowledge—that is, into literature" (504). The lack of national traditions of scientific thought in Latin America and the region's scarce production of scientific knowledge is raised by the Venezuelan intellectual Andrés Bello in his "Autonomía cultural de América," published in 1848. As a result of this perceived lack, Bello defends a "narrative" versus a "scientific" approach to history. Scientific understanding is useful where there is adequate information: "But when the history of a country does not exist except in scattered, incomplete documents, in vague traditions that must be collated and judged, the narrative method is obligatory" (45).[5] Other nineteenth-century intellectuals pushed the connection between national history and narrative even further. Doris Sommer points out that the Argentine writer/statesman Bartolomé Mitre went so far as to write a "manifesto promoting the production of nation-building novels" while at the same time he wrote in this genre (9).[6]

One area in which much of the project of nation-building in Latin America takes place is within literary discourse. Thus the relationships between Latin American women's writings and the national culture warrant careful examination. Which writers are perceived to play a role on the national political stage in Latin America bears directly on this inquiry. Examples of the writer-statesman abound in Latin America. Pedro Henríquez Ureña notes as much in his characterization of nineteenth-century Latin American writers: "Our men of letters were then, as a rule, also men of action. A number of them became presidents of republics. Many were cabinet ministers. Most were, at one time or another, members of congresses" (116). His *Literary Currents in Hispanic America* includes a page-long list of "men of letters" who were presidents of Latin American countries (243). Literary traditions that favor national works over those with supposedly personal themes have undoubtedly contributed to the inferior status of writings by women. As is the case with literature, in literary critical discourse, the critic's gender often determines whether a work is considered of broad interest. Marked as "feminine," women's writing as a whole is traditionally understood as personal and is therefore not of public significance simply because it is written by women. Here, we might think of Michel Foucault's notion of the "author function" and the social role that writers play within matrices of power.[7] In the present case, the gender marking of the text via the sex of its author determines how it is read and classified.[8] This strategy results in texts written by men being marked as "masculine" and therefore more likely to be of public significance than those written by women regardless of their content. In a move that equates personal experience with the life/history of the nation, the personal when marked as masculine is often seen to be representative in terms of the nation and therefore public. By contrast, the personal when marked as feminine is seen as private.

The positioning of men's autobiographies and biographies provides an obvious example. Nineteenth-century Latin American writers/statesmen equated autobiographies and biographies with the histories of their nations.[9] Domingo F. Sarmiento includes his own life story as national example when he writes in his *Recuerdos de provincia,* published in 1850, "The biography is the most original book South America has to offer in our time, and the best material for history" (318–319). Moving to the twentieth century, José Vasconcelos, at least by the title of his autobiography, *Ulises criollo: La vida del autor escrita por él mismo* (four volumes, 1935–1939), confers on himself the status of mythic hero: "The title that I have given the whole work is explained by the contents. A destiny rising like a comet, suddenly blazing into life, then extinguishing itself during long periods of darkness, and the turbulent atmosphere of present-day Mexico, justify the analogy with the *Odyssey.*"[10]

In the field of literary criticism, emphasis on national literary history locates women's writings about literature and culture as outside the national interest while locating very similar writings by men within the field of literary criticism.[11] As an example of the power of gender marking in this process, imagine how the following excerpt of a literary essay would be classified had it been marked as feminine:

> He has stretched out his arms and has embraced with them the secret of life. From his body, light basket of his winged spirit, he ascended between painful labors and mortal anxieties, to those pure peaks, on which are outlined, as a prize for the zeal of the traveler, the tunics

embroidered with the stellar light of infinite beings. He has felt that mysterious overflowing of the soul in the body that is a solemn venture and fills the lips with kisses and the hands with caresses and the eyes with weeping and seems like the sudden swelling and brimming of Nature in spring.[12]

José Martí's emotional and sensual description of Ralph Waldo Emerson is no less "personal" or "flowery" or "intimate," all adjectives customarily employed to describe the feminine, than any literary commentary written by the women authors studied here, yet his work will be considered "literary journalism," rather than personal reflection, by literary historians like Pedro Henríquez Ureña, who writes, "His style developed and matured slowly; it attained its fullness when he was nearly thirty, and from then on no insignificant line flowed from his pen, whether in a bit of journalistic news or in a private letter" (163).

The process of choosing what should constitute public knowledge versus what should be considered private thought is in play when such critical determinations are made. As we acknowledge the particularities of the situation of women writers in Latin America and examine these categories, we might keep in mind that most feminist theory addressing itself to the issues facing women writers in the First World presents difficulties for the way it understands the position of the writer in society. For example, certain feminist theories are inadequate for dealing with how race and class oppression affect women's lives both within and outside the borders of First World nations.

Recent Third World feminist theory has, in particular, called into question the previously uninterrogated distinction between the "public" and the "private" spheres. While a recognition of this distinction has been useful in certain feminist readings, it is potentially inappropriate in others. Specifically, the public/private binary is most relevant for middle- and upper-class white women. The politics of personal life can be differently defined for other groups because they do not live under the economic conditions that generate the public/private distinction. Transforming the familiar phrase, Aída Hurtado asserts in *The Color of Privilege: Three Blasphemies on Race and Feminism* that for women of color, the public is "*personally* political": "Welfare programs and policies have discouraged family life, sterilization programs have restricted reproductive rights, government has drafted and armed disproportionate numbers of people of Color to fight its wars overseas, and, locally, police forces and the criminal justice system arrest and incarcerate disproportionate numbers of people of Color" (18). Though

Hurtado is critiquing the public/private binary in terms of the experiences of women of color in the United States, the type of state intervention to which these women's "personal" lives are subjected has its unfortunate analogies all over Latin America. Furthermore, her analysis points to one of the potential pitfalls in criticism narrowly focused on gender: exclusive attention to gender politics can erase class and racial difference.

In a Latin American context, the comments directed by Domitila Barrios de Chungara to the chair of the Mexican delegation to an International Year of the Woman Tribunal in 1975 remain a sharp reminder of the dangers of such an erasure:

> Señora, I've known you for a week. Every morning you show up in a different outfit and on the other hand, I don't. Every day you show up all made up and combed like someone who has time to spend in an elegant beauty parlor and who can spend money on that, and yet I don't. I see that each afternoon you have a chauffeur in a car waiting at the door of this place to take you home and yet I don't. And in order to show up here like you do, I'm sure you live in a really elegant home, in an elegant neighborhood, no? And yet we miners' wives only have a small house on loan to us, and when our husbands die or get sick or are fired from the company, we have ninety days to leave the house and then we're in the street.
>
> Now, señora, tell me: is your situation at all similar to mine? Is my situation at all similar to yours? So what equality are we going to speak of between the two of us? If you and I aren't alike, if you and I are so different? We can't, at this moment, be equal, even as women, don't you think?(202–203)

Domitila's remarks chip away at the public/private distinction from the vantage point of someone who is not economically privileged enough to sustain a "private" sphere distinguishable from the "public." Her claims provide one example of how the public/private binary may break down over issues of class or race or occupation. The title of her book, *Let Me Speak! Testimony of Domitila, a Woman of the Bolivian Mines* (1978) points to a further potentially distancing difference between oral and written cultural traditions. *I, Rigoberta Menchú, an Indian Woman in Guatemala* (1984), another testimonial from a Latin American woman, provides further evidence of the complexities inherent to a discussion of the personal. Menchú's is a collective narrative in which she emphasizes her voice as part of a plurality of voices comprised of the lived experiences of her cultural community. In her latest book, *Crossing Borders* (1998), Menchú points out how such forms of narration may be misappropriated in the contemporary publishing world. Ethnologist Elisabeth Burgos Debray holds the copyright to *I, Rigoberta Menchú*. After many years of silence, Menchú is now speaking out about her loss of power over her own story: "In those days I was innocent and naive. When I wrote that book, I simply did not know the commerical rules. I was just happy to be alive to tell my story. I had no idea about an author's copyright. . . . I am grateful to my Creator that I am alive, and I hope I can still finish the story, and regain the rights to that important part of the patrimony of my people, *Ixem Uleew*. It should belong to no one but them and Guatemala" (114–115).

The authors studied in this book are middle- and upper-class women. Still, I would argue that the public/private distinction should be interrogated for women in these groups as well. I turn now to two recent studies that take somewhat different approaches to this and other issues around women's writing: Debra Castillo's *Talking Back: Toward a Latin American Feminist Literary Criticism* (1992) and the Seminar on Women and Culture in Latin America's *Women, Culture, and Politics in Latin America* (1990). Though neither deals explicitly with women as cultural critics, both address the position of women writers in Latin America.

In the first chapter of her work, titled "Toward a Latin American Feminist Literary Practice," Castillo presents the reader with an "only slightly hyperbolic statement"—"Latin American women do not write" (27). On this depend other "truisms" of "standard Latin American literary history": "Latin American women certainly do not write narrative. What little they do write—poetry, mostly—deserves oblivion. What narrative they produce, straightforward neorealist domestic fiction, does not stand up to comparison with the work of the great male writers of the Boom and after and is mercifully relegated to a mere footnote" (26). Castillo obviously does not believe the "truisms" she has articulated for us. They nonetheless frame her arguments and represent that to which she "talks back" as the title of her book suggests. Because she construes and constrains her arguments in this way, she must then account for those women who *do* write:

> The occasional *exceptions*—Western-trained and European-oriented women such a María Luisa Bombal in Chile, Elvira Orphée, Victoria and Silvina Ocampo in Argentina, the Puerto Ricans Rosario Ferré and Ana Lydia Vega, the Brazilian Clarice Lispector, or the Mexicans Elena Garro, Margo Glantz, Barbara Jacobs, and Elena Poniatowska (whose non-Hispanic-sounding last names are almost too suggestive)—neatly

demonstrate the point, but they represent something of a conundrum in traditional literary histories. (my italics 26–27)

Castillo does not explain what she means by "Western-trained" or just how these exceptions "neatly demonstrate the point." Her tone signals that she is displeased with the space prescribed for these women, yet her construction of this scene traps the writers she mentions in an absolute. From this position, she must devote considerable energy to reacting to traditional literary history.

A parallel observation could be made about the way in which Castillo frames her book. *Talking Back* begins and ends with a "recetario." By bracketing her text this way, the author invokes the traditionally feminine-marked space of the kitchen. Her *recetario* doesn't contain recipes, but rather quotations around the connections between women, cooking, creation, and eating. The *recetario*, Castillo writes, "suggests the common language, but also demonstrates that recipe sharing has a sinister as well as a celebratory side. The recipe serves as an index of female creative power; it also describes a giving of the self to appease another's hunger, leaving the cook weakened, starving" (xiv). Her suggestion that recipes hold out the possibility of a common language for women signals what Castillo herself describes as a utopian and nostalgic view. Though she uses the recipe as a model for feminine discourse: "at last, we dream, a common ground for positing a community of women" (xiv), her own subsequent warnings about the dangers of studying women outside specific historical and social contexts would seem to significantly diminish the benefits of such a strategy.

To accept Castillo's framework is to accept the kitchen as the "room of our own," as "the place where we write—or more often speak—our cooking secrets and our lives" (xiii). Despite her insightful observations, it is difficult to find within *Talking Back* a groundwork from which to study writing if we set aside the limiting frame of the kitchen. Castillo herself expresses an unfulfilled desire to arrive at a formula to describe Latin American women's writing in the first lines of her opening chapter: "Elaine Showalter's well-known essay 'Feminist Criticism in the Wilderness' contains an enormously attractive schematic summary of several major trends in recent feminist criticism. . . . The temptation to try to complement this formula with one strikingly pertinent to Latin America is almost overwhelming" (1). That Castillo should begin her book expressing a desire to emulate Showalter, the "great white mother" of feminist literary criticism, reveals the problems inherent to searching for an overarching critical paradigm for Latin American women's writings.[13]

Castillo worries that in using her own frame we might "obscure the historical problem of the limitation of women's exchange to certain levels—recipes, cosmetics—and its exclusion from others" (xiv). I worry that we might obscure women's exchange outside those areas, beyond what the private/public distinction allows us to see.

The approach to Latin American women's writing taken by the Seminar on Feminism and Culture in Latin America may prove more instructive. The insistence that our perception of women's relationship to culture not be limited to traditionally "feminine" activities unites the studies in *Women, Culture, and Politics in Latin America* by Seminar members Emilie Bergmann, Janet Greenberg, Gwen Kirkpatrick, Francine Masiello, Francesca Miller, Marta Morello-Frosch, Kathleen Newman, and Mary Louise Pratt. As such, their work pushes beyond the largest body of research on women which is driven by policy study and focuses on domestic activities and health: "The tendency to restrict culture and politics in these ways with respect to women reinforces a male elitism that claims serious intellectual, artistic, and political work as exclusive preserves of men" (vii). Perhaps it is their interdisciplinary collaborative approach to their work that permits the members of the Seminar to look beyond the traditional public/private distinction.[14] Their desire to (re)examine women's relationship to politics and culture lends their studies a sense of agency. They are not reacting, but acting to make/write the history of women's participation in literary culture and political life in Latin America. Underlying their work is a rejection of the notion of the exceptional female intellectual: "Sor Juana Inés de la Cruz has been seen as a unique phenomenon, an iconographic feminist presence, rather than as one of many women involved in a long tradition of engagement in Latin American culture" (1). This Sor Juana syndrome poses a challenge to Latin American literary studies.

The premises from which the Seminar's research emerges allow them to effectively combat the crippling and cramped notion of the exceptional woman writer who works in gender isolation. They have demonstrated the ways in which the public/private distinction is historically inaccurate, even as a means to describe the activities of white middle- and upper-class women in Latin America. In their research on the early twentieth century they show how women were engaging in public discourse in several areas. In her chapter in the Seminar's book, "Latin American Feminism and the Transnational Arena," as well as in her monograph, *Latin American Women and the Search for Social Justice* (1991), Francesca Miller investigates how women from the late nineteenth century to the present have participated in public, often international, organizations and conferences as part of a transnational feminist struggle. She argues, for example, that inter-American conferences held a special appeal for Latin American women who were disenfranchised within their national communities ("Latin" 10).[15] Female intellectuals in Latin American were alienated and excluded from the practice of politics in their countries. As a sign of this alienation and the ambiguity it produced in those women who wished to effect social change, Miller points to the case of the Venezuelan writer Teresa de la Parra (1890–1936).

In her speech "Influencia de la mujer en la formación del alma americana," given at an international conference of Latin American women authors in Bogotá in 1930 and published in her *Obra: Narrativa-Ensayos-Cartas,* Teresa de la Parra rejects both history and politics as the dirty work of men. De la Parra's critique of politics within her speech can be read as a political act in itself. Her disappointment with official history is understandable given that conferences such as the one at which she delivered this speech were not acknowledged as historical/political events. Miller documents the participation of Latin American women in numerous inter-American conferences, shattering historiographic assumptions implying that "feminist thought in Latin America is derivative and not sui generis" ("Latin" 11). Miller's research, like that of the Seminar participants studying print culture, suggests that examination of women's involvement in these conferences entails a rewriting of Latin American cultural history.

During the period in which the texts I examine are written (roughly 1920 to 1950), the field of literary production is dominated by men. The approach to literary and cultural criticism most employed in Latin America at this time is what has been referred to as "impressionistic." In his *A crítica literária no Brasil,* Wilson Martins describes the "família espiritual" of impressionistic criticism as the oldest and most popular in the history of Brazilian literary criticism (98). In the chronological chart Martins includes as an appendix to his text, the "impressionistic" tendency describes the greatest number of critics during this period in Brazil. While noting that impressionism in criticism became synonymous with dilettantism, Martins defends this "spiritual family" by arguing that all criticism is, in some way, subjective. The definition of impressionistic criticism he provides is taken from Jules Lematire: "he qualified his criticism as 'impressions sincéres notés avec soin'. Yet another school was implicitly born" (99). Much of this critical writing of the period takes the form of newspaper articles which are occasionally collected and reprinted as books. Histories of national literatures, especially in Brazil, Mexico, and Argentina, also appear, and in some rare cases, critics publish literary biographies of individual authors.[16] By mid-century, we begin to see texts treating the exercise of literary criticism itself, generally cataloguing and grouping critics either by nationality and/ or by approach.

A brief examination of the literary criticism of two well-known mid-century critics provides us with a sense of their primary concerns as well as their views on the work of the writers studied here.[17] Pedro Henríquez Ureña mentions Lúcia Miguel Pereira, Victoria Ocampo, and Gabriela Mistral in his *Literary Currents in Hispanic America*. The text is an intro-duction to Latin American literature originally presented as a series of lec-tures at Harvard University in 1940 and 1941. In his preface to the first edition (published in English), Henríquez Ureña describes his task as one of laying out "our 'search for expression'." The work, then, is a chronological tracing of what he sees as the main currents in that search. Miguel Pereira and Ocampo each appear once in a footnote in the last chapter of the book, titled "Problems of Today: 1920–1940." The note, to which I will return, follows a single paragraph on women writers in the body of the text that attempts to explain their absence as a group from the author's analysis: "It is perhaps significant that, with a very few exceptions, women were absent from the copious literary movement of the [eighteen] eighties and nineties; it was probably too impersonal for them" (186–187). According to Henríquez Ureña, when women did appear in literary movements they were rebels, not because they rejected traditional restrictions on women's activi-ties but, "they merely ignored them at the time of writing" (187). His com-ments are somewhat contradictory—these women do not openly reject their restricted roles, yet he claims they speak most often of "disillusion and thwarted lives" (187). For Henríquez Ureña, Gabriela Mistral is the greatest of these women writers for her voice of pity and counsel, "through her love of children, of mothers, of the poor, of the peasant, of the Indian and the Negro, of all the part of mankind that suffers" (187). His comments partici-pate in a tradition of writing about Mistral, to be discussed below, that positions her as a mother figure and ignores aspects of her work that do not conform to a maternal image.

While Henríquez Ureña has something to say about Mistral, the afore-mentioned footnote reveals that he has no comment on a long list of con-temporary women writers. In the page-long footnote, he mentions the poets María Eugenia Vaz Ferreira, Delmira Agustini, Alfonsina Storni and Juana de Ibarbourou, each of whose work he describes in one sentence. His next sentence is extremely telling: "There are hundreds of followers of these poets, especially in Argentina and Uruguay; at the same time, new types of women have appeared in our literature" (276). There is no analysis or de-scription of these "new types" who are authors, not female characters, as his wording could suggest. His statement is simply followed by a list of thirty-one women writers, grouped by nationality, which begins with Victoria Ocampo and includes Lúcia Miguel Pereira. Female poets, essayists, novelists, and short-story writers are grouped together and left undiscussed. The reader finds only mute evidence of their existence.

Women writers are given even less attention in the study of literary criticism. Their writing tends to be ignored and/or defined out of the endeavor altogether. In *La crítica literaria contemporánea* (1957), Enrique Anderson Imbert notes the lack of a work like Wilson Martins's *A crítica literária no Brasil* dealing with Spanish America and attempts to delineate the contemporary tendencies and methods of literary criticism in those countries (133). His text, written specially for university students (11), is divided into four chapters: "Disciplines that study literature," "Generalities about criticism," "Modes of studying criticism," and "Classification of the methods of criticism." After elaborating on the relationship between literary study and history, sociology, linguistics, pedagogy, and erudition, Anderson Imbert concludes his first chapter with an explanation of what distinguishes true literary criticism:

> All those disciplines study literature as instrument, as problem, as part of the general culture, but they leave something untouched: the judgment of value. No one but the critic attacks from that angle. Criticism judges whether a work is or is not literature; it judges the literary excellence of a work; it judges the hierarchy of its value. That which the critic has to tell us he can say in very few words: "this has value, this does not."[18]

The evocation of the juridical, the use of the terms "hierarchy" and "value," signal the authority and power attached to literary critical practice as Anderson Imbert describes it. What he reserves as the exclusive domain of literary criticism after having carefully detailed how other disciplines can be useful to literary study is this power to judge, hierarchize, and assign value. He is adamant about the literary critic's role, repeating in the conclusion of the same passage, "Let us pay attention to those few words that the critic has for us, 'this has value, this does not,' they are irreplaceable" (27). Anderson Imbert doesn't deny that literary criticism can be "improvisado" and "irresponsable": he simply reminds us that the same is true in other fields. In case he should have to defend his endeavor and so that he is "prepared to show his credentials," the section titled "La axiología del crítico" contains two pages of questions concerning the critical process that the literary critic should be ready to tackle (38–41). The reader of Anderson Imbert's book is left with the impression that the field of literary criticism is embattled and that the critic must always be on the defensive.

Only five Spanish American women critics appear in *La crítica literaria contemporánea*: María Rosa Lida de Malkiel, Ana María Barrenechea, María Hortensia Lacau, Emma Susana Speratti Piñero, and Concha Meléndez. Criticism was not a woman's world in 1957. Little had changed in the nearly one hundred years that had passed since Gertrudis Gómez de Avellaneda wrote in 1860:

> If . . . a woman is still excluded from the temple of serious knowledge, don't think for a moment that her acceptance in literature and the arts has been a fact of many centuries' duration: oh, no! here, too, the field has been disputed inch by inch by blind masculine adherence to one idea. Even today she is regarded there as an intruder and a usurper and is consequently treated with certain animosity and distrust, which is most visible in the distance at which she is kept from the *bearded* academies. Let this adjective pass, dear sister readers, because it flowed naturally from our pen on mentioning those illustrious associations of literary types whose primary and most important attribute is *having a beard*.[19]

Anderson Imbert would seem to have firsthand experience in this process of maintaining the bearded exclusivity of the literary and artistic field. He and Henríquez Ureña and many other male critics establish who the *hombres de letras* are based on their authority. Thus when José Martí uses a "feminine" style to talk about Emerson, his status as a man of letters is never in question. In this context, what is uncomfortably recognized as the "subjective" nature of literary criticism is seen as weakness in criticism produced by women, though it is perfectly acceptable when it comes from men.[20]

In discussions of women critics, clusters of issues emerge that impact the significance of the writing undertaken by them: the influence of cultural nationalism; the complex interplay of gender and class and their relationship to authorial power; the pervasiveness of eurocentric norms in defining cultural production. These issues inflect the various ways in which the three women of this study produce cultural knowledge. They also serve to help marginalize or erase the presence of women within masculinist discourses on Latin American cultural production. This study attempts to contest this erasure by spotlighting the manner in which these pioneering women produced their critical acts.

2

Lúcia Miguel Pereira and the Era(c)ing of Brazilian National Literature

Establishing a career quite distinct from that of other Latin American women who might be included in Henríquez Ureña's category of *hombres de letras,* Lúcia Miguel Pereira created a name for herself by publishing book-length works of literary criticism. She also wrote newspaper articles and reviews critiquing the literary production of her time that have only recently been collected under the titles *A leitora e seus personagens: seleta de textos publicados em periódicos (1931–1943), e em livros* (1992) and *Escritos da maturidade: seleta de textos publicados em periódicos (1944–1959)* (1994). Miguel Pereira is best known for her literary history *Prosa de ficção: de 1870 a 1920* (first published in 1950) and her literary biographies of Machado de Assis (1936) and Gonçalves Dias (1943). These books, per se, have not been the subject of previous study though they have been cited regularly by literary critics. Indeed, several editions of *Prosa de ficção* and *Machado de Assis* were published during Miguel Pereira's lifetime, and both were republished as recently as 1988. Ironically, in order for Miguel Pereira to assert her voice as a woman and a literary critic, she was required to participate in a discourse that served to erase women's voices. As a result, her critical work tends to erase women's voices from Brazilian literary historical discourse. Appropriately, Miguel Pereira requested that her own papers be burned upon her death; after she and her husband died together in a plane crash in 1959, all of her unpublished writings were destroyed.

Her publications remain remarkable for several reasons. Hers is the only such literary criticism produced by a woman in its time, and so represents a singular woman's voice in a field dominated by men. Simultaneously, and perhaps influencing why her work was (and is) well received, women writers are almost entirely absent from Miguel Pereira's literary histories. In this way, her critical work can be treated as normative and non-tendentious. Finally, despite the fact that it remains in print and is widely cited by other critics, Miguel Pereira's critical work is not studied in the contemporary histories of Brazilian letters. For example, Alfredo Bosi in *História concisa da literatura brasileira*, Antônio Cândido in *Formação da literatura brasileira*, and Wilson Martins in *A crítica literária no Brasil*, among others, cite her critical work without analyzing its worth or its merit.

While each of these issues is striking, for my purposes, the most relevant aspect of Miguel Pereira's literary criticism is its inattention to Brazilian women writers. In light of this absence, it is interesting to read Miguel Pereira's relatively unknown novels. They all focus on and highlight the consciousness of a female protagonist. In fact each is a fiction of female development. Taken together, they form a series of women's *bildungsromane*. As a group, these four texts embody Lúcia Miguel Pereira's fascination with the experiences of women and the shape of female lives as, through fiction, she explores issues of gender roles and sexuality.

Read in the light of her fiction and its preoccupation with the problems and politics of gender, Miguel Pereira's critical work is peculiarly silent. It may be possible to read her critical writing at a slant, so to speak. One may look toward other issues—such as race and class—which take a dominant place in her texts as a means by which her concern with gender becomes displaced. Race and class clearly do engage her critical imagination because these issues are central to the public discourse on Brazilian national identity. Gender, and more specifically gender inequality, does not take this kind of central role.

Miguel Pereira's novels are overrun by a clearly articulated concern with gender and its inequalities. In taking some time to review the contours of these forgotten fictions we may come to an understanding of where and how her concerns with issues of gender manifest themselves. Significantly, these concerns do not overtly work their way into her critical texts. Those texts arise out of a public discourse dealing with national identity and national culture. The space of national discourse is one not occupied by women. By contrast, the creative space forms a private location in which asymmetrical gender relations can be examined. In listening to Miguel Pereira's creative voice, one understands that the erasure of gender in her critical work becomes a form of displacement, a displacement undertaken in order to participate in the male-dominated discourse on Brazilian national culture.

Miguel Pereira's novels thematize issues central to women's movements through and against restrictive social and familial structures. Her work details the events significant to women of a certain social privilege and is interesting in terms of its class issues in addition to the attention she pays to gender and its construction and significance within systems of social order. Yet her extensive creative writing has been largely ignored. The novels—which received scant critical notice when they were published and have long been out of print—are four: *Maria Luiza* (1933), *Em surdina* (1933), *Amanhecer* (1938), and *Cabra-cega* (1954).[1] The only extensive reference to any of her novels is Cristina Ferreira Pinto's analysis of *Amanhecer* in *O bildungsroman feminino: quatro exemplos brasileiros* (1990).

Miguel Pereira's first novel, *Maria Luiza,* is a psychological portrait of a "perfect wife and mother" whose life is marked by isolation and ignorance. Maria Luiza's strict upbringing has afforded her little knowledge of the world outside the home. As children, she and her sister were under the constant watch of their mother and aunt. They did not attend school and had virtually no contact with other children for, as their father says: "girls are better off lacking education than roaming alone about the streets."[2] To his mind, education for the girls was too risky and would inevitably draw them away from the controlled atmosphere of his home. In response to her rigidly controlled youth, the adult Maria Luiza creates a perfectly ordered personal universe centered in a domestic space over which she herself has complete control. In her world of absolutes, the activities of "honest" women are highly circumscribed: "She could not believe women who would care for anything other than their house and children to be honest. She conflated in the same summary and inflexible condemnation both the stylish and the intellectuals."[3] The dissapproving tone of the authorial voice in *Maria Luiza* prompts the reader to take a critical view of the protagonist. We understand that she has constructed for herself a world that at once lacks style and intellectual stimulation.

That world begins to deteriorate when she and her husband, Artur, quarrel for the first time since their wedding. For Artur, life quickly returns to normal after their dispute. Maria Luiza, however, now experiences herself as separate from him and begins to doubt her own "perfection." Her ordered life quickly falls apart after she ventures an affair with her husband's best friend. The adulterous relationship provokes an intellectual awakening in her. Through reading and engaging in extensive discussions with her lover, she discovers a more creative and ambitious self: "an unknown woman awoke in her, a woman revolted by the sameness of life and vibrant with crazy aspirations."[4] For her lover, however, Maria Luiza is just one more sexual conquest, and the short-lived relationship ends abruptly.

The remainder of *Maria Luiza* documents the protagonist's changing psychological state as she comes to grips with the collapse of her world of moral absolutes and the loss of her lover. She feels victimized rather than valorized by her narrow upbringing that did not teach her how to cope with the values of others. She rails at her dumbfounded mother in her anger: "In short, hammered, ardent phrases she proclaimed her horror over the upbringing she had received; the crime of parents fabricating an imaginary world for their daughters, that sooner or later they will discover the deception of which they were victims."[5] In the end, Maria Luiza returns to her former domestic routine. Inwardly, however, she is transformed and is unable to make the kind of absolute moral judgments she had so easily entertained in the past. In this sense, Maria Luiza can be considered a precursor to many of the female protagonists in the work of Clarice Lispector who undergo similar psychological transformations within static surroundings.

Maria Luiza may also be read as a critique of the limited social interaction allowed Brazilian women of middle and upper classes in the early twentieth century. The novel calls attention to the double standard by which men are expected to have extramarital affairs while women are to remain uncritically devoted to their husbands. Maria Luiza's husband is only mildly bothered by his own occasional unfaithfulness. By contrast, Maria Luiza's one, brief, extra-marital relationship provokes in her a profound psychological crisis. Artur is judged by his business competence and other public activities while Maria Luiza's entire life is defined by her role within her private sphere as wife and mother. Her role is, to a great extent, defined by notions of purity and honesty, by ideas of private morality rather than public action. *Maria Luiza* is typical of most novels of female development. The protagonist has learned through an "awakening" about the interrelationships between herself, her family, and her society. Often, such awakenings end in death or disillusionment as the woman confronts societal limitations on her behavior (Rosowski 49).

Cecília, the protagonist in Miguel Pereira's *Em surdina*, is more aware of the world outside her home than is Maria Luiza. Ultimately, this knowledge does not help her lead a more independent life. As the novel opens, she turns down a marriage proposal from Jorge, a wealthy banker. While she allows her family to think that the young man is simply not up to her social standards, Cecília really rejects him because she is not willing to give up entirely on her childhood dreams of a heroic life as a warrior, a celebrated writer, an influential politician, a millionaire (12). She cannot reconcile herself to what she knows would be the highly circumscribed and uninspired life of a housewife.

Marriage, however, is what her family expects of her, and no one is interested in hearing about her concerns for her future. Her brother, assuming that she has turned down the proposal out of snobbery, suggests that she is lucky to have had a family-minded suitor: "Naturally, if he were to be crazy enough to want to marry, he would wind up like Jorge with some foolish girl who would prefer a down-and-out doctor to him. Marry ... bear a family ... Ugh ... What a horror! No woman was worth his freedom; one could have them, as many as he liked, without sacrificing a thing."[6] Here the novel reveals a common double standard. Cecília's brother can have women when he wishes and will not sacrifice his freedom for any one woman. Cecília, on the other hand, is expected to be grateful for the opportunity to be legally bound to a man whom she barely knows. Her reluctance calls our attention to the status of married women at that moment.

Historian June Hahner points out that even after the enactment of the republican Civil Code of 1916, married women in Brazil continued to be legally incapacitated: "Without her husband's authorization a wife could not accept or refuse an inheritance, exercise a profession, serve as a legal guardian, undertake litigation except to protect the family's communal property, or contract obligations which might lead to the alienation of the property" (82). No such restrictions were imposed on husbands. The Civil Code clearly had the effect of reinforcing the already prevalent notion that women's place was in the home supervising summarily "domestic" activities.

As we have seen thus far in Miguel Pereira's novels, particular attention is paid to the moral and sexual double standard whereby the same men who seek to confine women to a restricted household environment themselves engage in extramarital sexual relations. In another example, Cecília's father cites the threat that employment poses to her "honor" (and therefore to his reputation) as grounds to prohibit her from working outside the home. He lists every possible reason for his prohibition, including the breakdown of the family in post–World War I Europe (135–136). He views Cecília's desire to work primarily in terms of its potential negative effect on his life, although he is also concerned about her "losing herself." Meanwhile every member of his family is aware that he is engaged in a long-term extramarital affair with a "lost" woman of his own. Through the course of *Em surdina*, Cecília discovers that nearly all of the men in her family are implicated in this double standard.

Although it is not a consciously stated decision, Cecília slowly rejects the option of marriage for herself by refusing all proposals over a course of years. She would like to marry if marriage could ever involve a relationship between equals. She has, however, become painfully aware that this socially conventional institution does not provide a space for gender equality. As such, she prefers the relative freedom of caring for her father and his household.

Em surdina reveals that Cecília's option entails its own sacrifices. She must live through the lives of the other members of her family, piecing together scraps of their experiences to make a life of her own: "Was it made of the scraps of their existences? It didn't matter if with those scraps, with those leftovers, she managed to construct hers."[7] Her choice provides her with a life lived safely but at second hand in which all action is generated by others. Cecília envisions this existence as a kind of martyrdom through which she is raised "above herself, above her egotism" as she places the desires of others before her own (364). It becomes clear that this service will not render her any status or privilege. Just like the spinster aunt who helped raise Cecília and her siblings, she will pass quickly from memory despite her selfless service.

At the close of the novel we are forcefully reminded of the double standard which has led Cecília to choose this martyrdom over some unequal marriage. Her brother, while summing up the family's failures, argues that their father may only be considered "honest" because of his sex: "If it were he who had died and Mom had lived as he did, she would be a dishonest woman. Admitting his propriety, you must also admit a different moral for each sex, which implies the complete artificiality of the moral."[8] If ever the reader were in doubt, the author's conclusion clearly states the gender-based double standard in operation as well as its "artificiality."

Miguel Pereira's third novel, *Amanhecer,* again addresses gender inequality. Aparecida, its protagonist/narrator, is an intelligent and active young woman trapped in a small, stagnant town in the interior of the state of Rio de Janeiro. Despite the fact that her poor living conditions are attributable to her father, a failed entrepreneur who has gradually reduced the family to poverty, this woman vents her frustration on her mother, who for her represents the "miserable" domestic fate she is determined to escape. Rather than resign herself to repeating her mother's difficult and unhappy life, Aparecida briefly considers becoming a nun and then a teacher—the two professions traditionally considered acceptable for a woman in Latin America. Eventually she decides to move to the city to find a clerical job against her parents' wishes.

The female protagonist in this novel comes into conflict with both her family and herself over what she perceives her role as a woman to be. She is trapped between the desire to be independent and define her own life and the need to find the meaning of her life in others. This internal conflict is expressed in her simultaneous desires to be married and to escape women's traditional domestic roles. Though she would like to live and work independently in the city, Aparecida also dreams of her life as a carefree bride supported by a wealthy groom: "My betrothed would be [. . .] a medical student, and I would have servants and pretty dresses and I would read novels sitting in an easy chair."[9] Pushing her to be more independent and realistic, her friend Antônio encourages her to abandon these fantasies and learn to take care of herself: "He told me I should follow his example, that I shouldn't count on anyone, that I should fight, that I should work. I could not live on charity, nor could I bury myself alive in São José. Neither could I wait for an enchanted prince from heaven."[10] Deaf to his meaning, she is able to understand Antônio's advice only as a rebuff.

When she does break from her family and move to the city to work, Aparecida is unable to resolve her conflict about her role as a woman. Finding that psychologically she cannot cope with her freedom, she tries literally to give herself to Antônio, saying, "I will be your lover, Antônio, your servant, your slave."[11] Unable to escape the ideology of female inferiority, Aparecida feels that she must subordinate herself to a superior: "I only feel good in the company of people like that, the ones who overshadow me. Antônio is in the habit of saying that I need to humiliate myself and maintains that I have a sadistic streak."[12] Despite her wish for independence, by the end of the novel, she has traded one dependent situation for another.

Nonetheless, her life has changed in significant ways for as the title *Amanhecer* suggests, she has experienced a process of awakening. Through the course of the novel, constructed as her first-person memoir, she has become more self-aware. This is apparent in the narration through which she comments on the past with insights unavailable to her at the time of the events she is recalling. A later self commenting on a former self emerges in the following passage in which Antônio warns her against the hypocrisy of marriage and of the concept of female honor:

> Virginity—how embarrassed I was to hear that word!—and marriage were preconceptions. Bourgeois preconception, the notion of feminine honor. Pleasure is enjoyed as much by the girl as by the boy; there is no guilt for her nor responsibility for him. They should be partners, not giving import to things that had none. Love was very rare, and instinct very pressing.

Why connect one to the other? That's where sexual repressions with dire consquences came from. *I reconstructed his ideas more because I heard him repeat them many times later than because I understood them at the time.* (my emphasis)[13]

Though she was unable to at the time, Aparecida now writes from a position that understands Antônio's meaning. She has since learned about sexuality and pleasure.

With Aparecida, Lúcia Miguel Pereira creates a protagonist who does not accept the roles available to her as a woman in the early twentieth century: housewife, nun, teacher. Through the novel, we see her struggle against her own prejudices and those of her family and strive for her independence. Her story suggests the obstacles women faced (and continue to face) when they wished to move outside their traditional gender-based roles. That the protagonist finds she is unable to escape her need to be "owned" by a man speaks more to the pervasive power of patriarchy than to her psychological weakness. *Amanhecer* makes an argument for women's right to work in non-traditional occupations and, as do all of Miguel Pereira's novels, highlights the damaging effects of patriarchal structures.

In her last novel, *Cabra-cega*, Lúcia Miguel Pereira returns to the theme described in *Maria Luiza* as, "the crime of parents fabricating an imaginary world for their daughters."[14] *Cabra-cega*'s teenage protagonist, Ângela, is "protected" by her parents and older siblings who exclude her even from discussions of family matters. Old enough to recognize that all is not as her family pretends it is, Ângela is frustrated by her ignorance. She feels different from her schoolmates because of her living situation: she and her parents, grandmother, brother, and sister live in a luxurious house on a large estate while her grandmother's mentally ill sister, Aunt Regina, is confined to a smaller, run-down house concealed in a wooded area of the property. Ângela has never seen Regina and is not permitted to go near her house. Because her great-aunt often screams, no visitors are ever invited to the estate. Neither the fact of Regina's screams nor her existence is ever mentioned by Ângela's family, and so an air of secrecy and shame surrounds these circumstances. The title, *Cabra-cega,* suggests that Ângela's relationship to her family is like a game of blind-man's bluff. As the novel progresses, she slowly removes the blindfold.

By the close of *Cabra-cega* Ângela discovers the secrets her family has been keeping from her for many years: that her sister is a lesbian, that her now deceased grandfather raped his sister-in-law Regina, that a son who was born as a result of that rape was taken to an orphanage, and that her parents and grandmother are stealing and living off of Regina's inheritance.

After learning the ugly truth she decides to denounce her family to the police. She waits nervously for hours at the station to see a deputy and then loses her resolve and wanders into the street in an exhausted daze. She is lightly grazed by a car and finds herself telling her story to the driver who has stopped to help her. The man tries to convince her that her family, though they have overprotected her, is not as evil as she thinks. He suggests that she learn to take care of herself, enjoy life more by learning to lie as they do. She decides to begin by lying about her whereabouts that very afternoon: "To arrive home having come from the apartment of a stranger will be a private but complete, magnificent revenge. Doesn't each one of them have their secret, even grandmother? Well, she will have hers too."[15]

Finding her own view undermined yet again, this time by a stranger, Ângela relents. It is too difficult to carry on defending her moral stance while others (even strangers) either deny or trivialize her interpretation of events. Since no one will accept her interpretations, she will follow her family's example by not worrying about others and concentrating on self-gratification. Her family's control has finally caused her to rebel by emulating them through lying.

Ângela, like the female protagonists in each of Lúcia Miguel Pereira's novels, is portrayed as the victim of a cripplingly limited education. Through the course of the novels, Maria Luiza, Cecília, Aparecida, and Ângela all receive inadequate education. They all awaken to the societal limitations placed on them, and somehow come to terms with their new insights. Ângela will learn to lie and be more self-centered, Aparecida will be a slave to her man, Cecília will piece her life out of others' scraps, and Maria Luiza will return to her programmed domestic routine. These individual solutions can be read as failures in the face of an impossible task— combatting patriarchal ideology that restricts women to the private sphere by limiting their access to knowledge and public opportunity and forcing their financial dependency on men. Together the novels constitute an indictment of the social codes which severely restricted women in the early twentieth century and, to some extent, continue to do so today. As I have stressed in this brief overview, they are devoted thematically to a portrayal of women trapped in traditional gender roles of daughter, mother, wife. All of them reveal the damaging consequences of this confinement.

Miguel Pereira's literary themes are not typical for their time. In the 1930s and 1940s most Brazilian novels were written by men about men. Literature of this period was dominated by what is often referred to as "regionalismo," and this in turn by what is known as the "romance nordestino" or novel of the Northeast. The immense popularity of these novels has led the contemporary critic José Maurício Gomes de Almeida to argue that for many, the phrase "romance de 30" means "romance nordestino" (175–176). Some of the best-known Brazilian authors of the twentieth century—José Lins do Rego, Jorge Amado, Graciliano Ramos—published "romances nordestinos." José Lins do Rego's *Menino de engenho*, published in 1930, is often considered the first such novel. *Menino de engenho* opens his "ciclo da cana de açucar," a series of novels centering around the decline of the Northeastern sugar plantations and constituting a nostalgic recuperation of patriarchal plantation society. *Menino de engenho* is typical of the novels of this period not only in its regionalist theme, but in its treatment of women. In Lins do Rego's novel, as in others, sexual initiation with a female slave or subordinate house servant is presented as a normal, healthy part of the privileged Brazilian male's upbringing. Though it is true that a similar situation arises in *Cabra-cega*, nowhere is this apparently common practice discussed, as it is in Miguel Pereira's novel, from the perspective of a woman who recognizes its injustice. Nor is the gender-based double standard of such liaisons emphasized elsewhere in the way it is in her works.

Not surprisingly, other potentially more threatening women-centered topics such as lesbianism and abortion do not appear in the male-dominated canon of the period. Neither are they discussed in what little criticism of Miguel Pereira's novels has been published. In fact, in one of the few published commentaries on her novels, Temósticles Linhares completely misreads the protagonist's lesbian sister in *Cabra-cega*, ascribing her "problem" to an out-of-wedlock pregnancy rather than to her insistence on her sexual preference (409). Such willfull misreading reveals resistance to literary treatments of these issues. Patricia Galvão's once forgotten *Parque Industrial* (1933), another novel of the period that touches on lesbianism and abortion, provides a telling example of the silence with which these topics were met by the literary establishment until such recent publications as Bergmann and Smith's *¿Entiendes?: Queer Readings, Hispanic Writings* (1995), Molloy and Irwin's *Hispanisms and Homosexualities* (1998), and Foster's *Gay and Lesbian Themes in Latin American Writing* (1991) and *Sexual Textualities: Essays on Queer/ing Latin American Writing* (1997).

As her treatment of these issues indicates, what fundamentally distinguishes Lúcia Miguel Pereira's novels from those of her more widely read male contemporaries is her concern with women's lives and relationships within the traditional confines of the domestic sphere. Though they may be focused on one male character, or perhaps even be novels of male development, most of these other novels connect men's lives with historical events on a regional or national scale. José Lins do Rego documents the historical economic decline of the sugar plantations in his "cana de açucar" cycle; Jorge Amado traces the development of Bahia's cocoa producing region in his "ciclo do cacau." Érico Veríssimo, another widely read author of the period, traces a Brazilian family from the eighteenth through the twentieth century in his seven-volume series, O tempo e o vento. The history of this fictional family is depicted as intimately linked to political, economic, and other social forces—particularly wars and elections. In keeping with their focus on women, public events surface in Miguel Pereira's novels only as they affect the emotional life of her characters. Maria Luiza's worries about the revolution of 1930, for example, are depicted as a distraction from her domestic problems; no details of the events themselves are given. Veríssimo's novels, on the other hand, contain long historical/political tracts in both narration and dialogue.

It is not surprising that Miguel Pereira's novels have received very little critical attention. Virtually all Brazilian literary critics of her time were men (with the exception of the author herself), and her novels voice women's concerns. The silence which surrounded these writings may very-well derive from their focus on middle-class women's lives and the confinement to the domestic sphere that such emphasis entails; they are too dissimilar from the acclaimed novels of the period by Lins do Rego, Amado, Ramos, Veríssimo and others. Perhaps most significantly, they do not engage in a project that seeks to articulate national or regional Brazilian identity as does her literary criticism.

A brief look at the literary historical fate of one of Miguel Pereira's female contemporaries offers an intriguing juxtaposition. The novels of Rachel de Queiroz (1910–), the one canonized female novelist of the first half of this century, have claimed the attention of mainstream literary critics. Her critical success can be largely attributed to her inclusion within the group of Northeastern regionalist writers, an identification spurred by her first novel, O quinze (1930), a novelistic account of the Northeastern drought of 1915. Stressing the absolute centrality of the Northeast in her work, the author herself asserted in an interview upon her induction to the Brazilian Academy of Letters, "It wasn't I who entered the Academy, it was the people of Ceará."[16]

Despite the level of recognition she has achieved, even Rachel de Queiroz's success must be qualified. As its first female member, she was not inducted into the Academy until 1977, forty-seven years after the publication of O quinze (which, as of 1997, was in its sixty-seventh Brazilian edition) and coincidentally, forty-seven years after the first unsuccessful nomination of a female candidate to that exclusive institution.[17] By that time de Queiroz had published a tremendous body of work with a regional emphasis on Brazil's Northeast.[18] The initial disbelief with which her publishing success was met by mainstream writers and critics has been explored by Heloísa Buarque de Hollanda in her essay on the author's entrance into the Academy, "A roupa da Rachel: um estudo sem importância," in which she quotes the remarks of Graciliano Ramos:

> O *quinze* fell suddenly there in the middle of '30 and wounded the spirits more than José Américo's novel for it was by a woman, and what really caused dread, by a young woman. Was it really by a woman? I didn't believe it. Having read the book and seen the picture in the newspaper, I shook my head: there is no one with this name. It's a prank. A girl like that writing a novel! It must be the pseudonym of some bearded type.[19]

The novel was so different in its style from those of de Queiroz's female contemporaries that Ramos and others have admitted they could not believe it was written by a woman. Arguably Brazil's most successful female novelist, de Queiroz openly rejected the feminist movement in her declarations as the first woman to enter the Brazilian Academy of Letters.

Her individualist stance is not surprising given the social context in which she began her publishing career. In early-twentieth-century nationalist discourse, women were restricted to the domestic, the private, the personal. Consequently, a concern for women—their role, their power or powerlessness—does not easily find its place within the development of a national literary critical discourse. While the fictional, the creative, the imaginative may have been an appropriate space for a few women's voices, the historical, the political, the critical was not. As Lúcia Miguel Pereira herself notes, "The novelist—who in this is similar to the poet, although their reactions diverge—needs to receive life, let himself be penetrated by it, in a passivity like that of gestation. There is something feminine in his attitude and something masculine in that of the critic."[20] The novelist is passive, accepting, feminine. The literary critic, on whom the writer often depends for success, is active, assertive, masculine.

As a literary critic, Lúcia Miguel Pereira, like most of her predecessors and contemporaries, was interested in asserting the development of a uniquely Brazilian literary tradition. Nineteenth-century Brazilian literary critics had taken as their primary task the definition and delineation of a true Brazilian literature, distinct and separate from Portuguese literature. Building on the work of their predecessors, Miguel Pereira and other critics of the first half of the twentieth century continued to focus on the anxiety-provoking question of a national literature. In the introduction to her critical survey of Brazilian literature, *Prosa de ficção: de 1870 a 1920,* Miguel Pereira makes the case for a historically relative critical approach.[21] Due to the unstable nature of the young Brazilian nation, she argues, Brazilian writing will not hold up to a comparison with European writing. It can only be fairly evaluated if one emphasizes the circumstances of its production: "Perhaps when one studies an incipient literature, as is the case, one can and should, without lapsing into historicism, attribute greater importance to the circumstances of time and environment."[22] Her suggestion signals a widely held belief in a superior European literature against which "incipient" literature, like that of Brazil and other Latin American countries, should be judged.

While she analyzes the works of various individual authors in *Prosa de ficção,* Miguel Pereira's overall concern in this book is with the literary tendencies and developments revealed through her historical approach to Brazilian literature produced from the end of the romantic period to just prior to modernism. Since her primary goal is to sketch a broad portrait of the national literature of that time, there appears to be little room for women's writings in her discussion. After all, from her perspective, the central figures are the great forefathers of Brazilian literature. From this traditional point of view, women have contributed nothing to the national literature.

Miguel Pereira's comments on women writers in *Prosa de ficção* are concentrated in her two-page discussion of Júlia Lopes de Almeida (1862–1934), one of the most prolific of all Brazilian writers. Rather than analyze Lopes de Almeida's numerous works, as she does in the sections on individual male authors, Miguel Pereira uses this space to dismiss all women writers of the period. Since many of these authors' works are lost, she argues, we must accept the judgment of their contemporary literary critics who ignored them: "And even to one or another remembered by the critics of the time . . . one can't dedicate space in the literary history."[23] Replicating the silence with which the works of these earlier women writers were originally met, in her own criticism, Miguel Pereira offers no other explanation for why they do not deserve a place in Brazilian literary history. It is, her work implies, simply understood that they do not belong. As for Júlia Lopes de Almeida, the only woman meriting her own—albeit very brief—section, she finds her work unoriginal, too impersonal, and not very Brazilian (259–260). She makes these claims without providing textual support from Lopes de Almeida's works, a strategy she regularly employs when making claims about the male authors she critiques.

Miguel Pereira's treatment of women's writing within the landscape of Brazilian national literature is revealing. For on one hand, she argues that one must maintain a critical relativism in relation to Brazil's literature as a nascent literature. The circumstances of its production must be emphasized. On the other hand, she is not willing to extend her critical relativism to women's writings in the way she does to the national literature.

This is not to say that Miguel Pereira's criticism does not address the presence of women within literary texts. In fact, some of her readings in *Prosa de ficção* suggest that male authors fall short when it comes to an adequate portrayal of women. She criticizes naturalist writers, for example, for presenting too much of a one-dimensional view of women. For the naturalists, women serve only as vessels of reproduction. And she notes that Lima Barreto, in particular, constructed his male characters with much more depth than his female characters (299). Her remarks, however, do not extend beyond pointing out what she feels are unrealistic characterizations. By and large, women (and the one individual female author mentioned above) receive scant attention in *Prosa de ficção*.

To whom, then, does Miguel Pereira devote most of her critical attention? *Prosa de ficção* contains twenty-three author studies. Twenty-one of these range in length from two to fifteen pages. By contrast, Machado de Assis is discussed for forty-eight pages, and Lima Barreto is treated in a thirty-page section. These two authors are, interestingly, the two mestizo writers included in her study.[24] Thus one approach to the seeming discrepancy between the centrality of women's concerns in Lúcia Miguel Pereira's novels and their marginalization in her critical writings is to suggest that, within her literary criticism, issues of gender are displaced by issues of race. We might find in her critique of the significance of race to the literary scene some form of allegory which might help us understand her position on that other greatly disempowered group: women.

In addition to *Prosa de ficção*, Miguel Pereira published biographies of the two great patriarchs of Brazilian literature—Machado de Assis and Gonçalves Dias. In all three works, she devotes considerable space to the details of the authors' racial heritages. Establishing Machado de Assis's racial makeup is so important that in the preface to the third edition of *Machado de Assis: estudo crítico e biográfico,* she must reiterate his color in light of new biographical evidence. Though he had previously been thought to be a *mulato,* Machado's baptism record revealed that his mother was white. Miguel Pereira argues, however, that the discovery is not significant: "In the case of the descent of Machado de Assis, the paternal is infinitely more important than the maternal. What would mark him forever, what would condition his reactions to men and to life, would be the color he inherited from the father, and that the mother can have attenuated without, however, leaving it less visible."[25] Since race is the starting point for her analysis of Machado's life and works, his status as a writer of color must be reasserted in the face of the new evidence of his white ancestry.

The first sentence of *A vida de Gonçalves Dias* reveals a similar highlighting of race: "After having written a book about Machado de Assis, I was assailed by [. . .] the temptation to write another about Gonçalves Dias, to study our first great poet after studying our greatest novelist, to reunite in some sense those two admirable mestizos."[26] From the outset, Miguel Pereira calls attention to the race of her famous biographical subjects that, like their literary achievements, forms a link between them. She goes on in the first pages of the biography to give a detailed account of Gonçalves Dias's racial background, including a collection of verbal descriptions of his mother intended to support the conclusion that she was *cafuza*. [27] Like her literary historian predecessors Sílvio Romero and José Veríssimo, whom she cites for support, Miguel Pereira asserts that "his temperament is explained by the combined inheritance of the three races—the Portuguese from the father, the Indian and Black from the mother."[28] Her recourse to the myth of Brazil's three founding races marks her place within a romanticized literary historical tradition established in the nineteenth century.

Miguel Pereira also grounds on race her argument for the similarity between Machado de Assis and Lima Barreto, whom she calls "our two greatest dead novelists."[29] Her emphasis lies not on common influences or similarities in literary styles. She even concurs to a degree with Barreto's insistence that there is a great difference between his work and that of the older master. Favoring race over other points of convergence, her work stresses the fact that both writers need to realize themselves through their novels, "to translate their position in the face of life."[30] They are *mulato* writers experiencing chronic health problems who, she suggests, use their writing as a way of compensating for "deficiencies" in their lives:

> And the deficiencies from which they suffered must have brought together the man who wrote "hiding what he felt so as not to debase himself" and the one who did so "with much fear of not saying everything he wanted and felt, without calculating whether he was debasing or exalting himself."

If he did not depart, like Machado, from extreme poverty, Lima Barreto was also a mulatto, and this signified much, unfortunately, in this our paradoxical land of mestizos. If he wasn't like Machado, completely self-taught, he could not, as the head of his family and twenty-one years of age, by virtue of his father's illness, finish the studies he had begun in the Polytechnic School. If he did not suffer like Machado from nervous illness, his alcoholism—which must have been tied to the father's madness—more than once left him at the brink of insanity.[31]

In her exploration of their "deficiencies," we might be tempted to read into Miguel Pereira's treatment of race some parallel to the problems of gender and writing. Within a nationalist literary project at that time, coming to terms with race mixture was a necessary step in thinking through national identity in Brazil given that *mestizagem* was inevitable. Dealing with gender issues was clearly not central to that same project. Looking for some parallel between Miguel Pereira's engagement with race and her engagement with gender is complicated by the fact that she eventually comes to conflate race not with the issue of gender but of class. While she takes a great deal of care to establish their mixed racial backgrounds, she employs the authors' race as a marker by which to locate them socio-economically. Machado de Assis was able to capture the depth of life in Rio de Janeiro due to the fact that he was born into a low social class. Miguel Pereira argues that his insights derive "not from being mestizo, but from having come from the people, from having belonged to different social strata."[32] Machado's novels are superior to those of his white counterparts because his economic position during his youth provided him with a broader exposure to the diverse population of the city. Her strategy accounts for Machado's difference and literary achievements in a de-racialized manner.

After carefully defining Gonçalves Dias's race in physical terms in *A vida de Gonçalves Dias,* Miguel Pereira notes that he seldom mentioned his racial heritage himself. The poet studied Amerindians and might have played-up his own Amerindian ancestry, but he avoided biographical explanations: "It is not impossible that into his indianism had entered the intimate impulse to cling to the Indian, in a transposition to the personal plane of that which happened on the national plane—the desire to exalt a race about which one bragged, concealing the desire to forget the other race, the one that could humiliate."[33] While it was, in theory, acceptable to be Amerindian, it was socially disadvantageous to be Black. I say "in theory" because there is no evidence that it was actually socially advantageous to be an Amerindian in the nineteenth century; quite to the contrary. The *image* of an imagined, ancestral Amerindian, one who represented America's native difference but was not threatening to European cultural values, was idealized.

Despite her lengthy discussion of Gonçalves Dias and race, Miguel Pereira concludes that he was really most concerned about his illegitimate birth. The stigma of illegitimacy, rather than his race, drove him to avoid all discussion of his background: "The racial inferiority that he could compensate for through pride in being a descendent of the original owners of the land must have been less painful than the social inferiority that only through his own effort was he able to counterbalance."[34] Here, as in her analysis of the life of Machado de Assis, Miguel Pereira argues that class—in this case the diminished social standing conferred by illegitimacy—was more important to the author's self-understanding (and by extension, ours of him) than race. Gonçalves Dias has only his "self-value" to compensate for the unfortunate circumstances of his birth.

As Miguel Pereira contemplates Gonçalves Dias's exposure to Amerindian culture, it is not the fact that he was of Amerindian descent and experienced that culture as relevant to his life, but rather, its mere physical proximity during his youth that explains, for her, why he was drawn to study Amerindians as an adult. She describes in *A vida de Gonçalves Dias* how the poet spent the first years of his life physically surrounded by Amerindians and Afro-Brazilians: "Aside from his mother, he would see only [. . .] the Blacks from the cotton plantations and the tame Indians, makers of the clay pots used in his home, with whom he became familiar from early on."[35] In a replication of the common nineteenth-century views on race to which she has previously alluded, Miguel Pereira herself ignores any possible influence of Afro-Brazilian culture on his formation and asserts that Gonçalves Dias must have played with Amerindian objects and learned Amerindian words when, as a boy, he moved to the Northeastern village of Caxias. She cites the travel narrative of J. B. von Spix and C. F. P. von Martius for ethnographic detail:

> Caxias must have been more of a clearing than a town, full of Blacks, hillbillies, tame Indians [. . .] in bands in the streets "in complete primitive nudity and savagery," trading with its inhabitants "pieces of clothing, hatchets, knives and all manner of trifles" for "big balls of wax, feathers of beautiful colors and delicately sculpted bows and arrows."

As a boy, Gonçalves Dias must have played with those indigenous instruments, he must have learned many words from the savages who were his familiars. He would drink water from the clay pots they made; he would see his mother store the tidbits she cooked in gourds, some smooth, others of pretty colors; he would sleep wrapped in the cozy fiber or cotton hammocks; he would see the indigenous *tipití* used in the kitchen to make flour. He would certainly hear about *Tapuais, Timbiras, Tupís,* Indian wars; he would know they inhabited the woods he saw in the distance.[36]

Despite the reference to von Spix and von Martius, no documentation is offered to suggest that the above domestic scene existed anywhere other than in Lúcia Miguel Pereira's imagination. The description, however, reveals her positioning of Gonçalves Dias vis-à-vis Amerindian culture: he is surrounded by Amerindian artifacts and learns Amerindian words, but he is not within their culture. The "real" Amerindians are positioned outside, in the *matas.*

The distancing of Gonçalves Dias from Amerindian culture supports Miguel Pereira's assertion that the poet was more concerned with his illegitimacy than his racial identity. With her emphasis on social class as opposed to race, the notion emerges from Miguel Pereira's criticism that Machado de Assis, Lima Barreto, and Gonçalves Dias were great writers because they were able to improve their social standing. Her portrayals suggest they left little behind in their ascent to literary heights beyond their conditions of poverty. In the biography, Miguel Pereira depicts Machado de Assis as deserving of admiration for his ability to rise up from a lowly birth to attain a place of respect in high (white) society. He becomes an individual who, through hard work, manages to lift himself from his impoverished origins. A similar pattern emerges in the biography of Gonçalves Dias, though he is understood as having benefitted from the higher social position of his father. Miguel Pereira does not suggest that the authors' social ascent is achieved without any sacrifices, however, and here we touch again on the question of gender.

As she traces their careers, Miguel Pereira calls attention to the fact that Machado de Assis abandoned his stepmother and that Gonçalves Dias abandoned his mother. With phrases such as "he violently severed ties with the past [. . .] not wanting [. . .] to have constantly before his eyes that specter of a painful childhood, he abandoned the poor mulatta" and "In order to rise in social class he had to sacrifice his stepmother," she appears to simultaneously criticize their behavior and to suggest its necessity.[37] Though depicted as violent, the abandonment is eventually understood as essential to the success of their careers: the non-white mother figure must be sacrificed for upward mobility. By their mention, Miguel Pereira has raised the possibility of the importance of these women in their sons' lives. In describing Machado de Assis's relationship to his wife, Carolina, she carries this possibility much further. Carolina is the subject of chapter seven of *Machado de Assis,* which bears her name as its title and stresses the importance of her help to Machado in the editing of his manuscripts. Such attention to her role is an uncommon, and I think laudable, attempt to give this woman credit for her literary efforts.

Lúcia Miguel Pereira's treatment of Carolina, however, does not necessarily reveal some overall commitment on her part to recover and value women's literary contributions. Carolina was white and Portuguese, making her influence on the darker Machado acceptable and even culturally desirable. Miguel Pereira suggests that the "educated and refined" Carolina filled in some of Machado's "cultural lacunae," that she led him to read English writers, and that "The very purity of language of our greatest prose writer may have suffered the influence of contact with that cultivated Portuguese woman."[38]

Miguel Pereira indicates that Machado's stepmother also had an important influence on him. From her perspective, however, the marked differences between Maria Inês and Carolina outweighed their similarities as women and supporters of Machado:

> Without doubt, generous as she was, Carolina would not have refused to receive in her home the mulatta who had been so good to her beloved Machado—if he had asked her to. But certainly it was he who preferred the separation, and perhaps even had hidden from his wife the influence of Maria Inês in his life. He would fear the presence of that dissonant note in his interior harmony. And, if he acted poorly in the moral sense, very poorly, pyschologically, he was on the mark. Not to mention the constant humiliation this irrefutable proof of his modest origins would be for him. How could the educated Carolina and the humble Maria Inês relate to each other? Both would be uncomfortable, and he even more so than the two of them.[39]

What separates and defines Carolina and Maria Inês for Miguel Pereira is "culture." Maria Inês's lack of "culture" is marked by her race—she is referred to here and elsewhere as "the mulatta." She is an unpleasant reminder of Machado's *mulatice,* his "mulatto-ness," and the poverty and illness with which it is connected.

In a similar fashion, Miguel Pereira introduces Gonçalves Dias's mother, Vincência, into her text as "a mestiza, a poor, humble, illiterate girl," and nearly all further mention of her contains the qualifier/marker "mestiza" (*Gonçalves* 10). She appears to criticize the treatment of non-white women like Vicência by men like Gonçalves Dias's father, who abandoned her for a white wife, when she asks, "what Portuguese man would not get together, in the early days, with the women of color? The skin tone matters little; blacks, mulattas, or copper-skinned, all will do, all are submissive, affectionate and economical—all are women and servants."[40] Her tone would suggest she considers such treatment of women lamentable. Yet, as she goes on to describe the "realistic" relationship between Gonçalves Dias's parents, Vincência emerges as a "primitive" with no personal agency: "What would she do, the poor thing, with her hot mestiza body and her tenderness of a primitive, if she did not get together with a new companion?"[41] The suggestion that Vicência's actions are determined by her "hot mestiza body" reveals another point at which Miguel Pereira's concern for women and her ideas about race are in conflict. The biography conveys the notion that though morally one should not abandon or "sacrifice" one's illiterate or "primitive" mother, it is both understandable and necessary to do so for reasons of social mobility.

Beyond the depiction of the origins (specifically the mothers) of these mixed-race authors as culturally and racially inferior, Miguel Pereira makes an implicit connection between their racial backgrounds and illness or decay. This position is clearly informed by nineteenth-century European theories on race, and in particular the notion that racial mixture inevitably leads to biological degeneration. An example of this type of racially determinist thinking is evident in the language Miguel Pereira uses to describe Machado's return to his old neighborhood. In considering what Machado must have felt as he returned sometime prior to when he married and completely abandoned his stepmother she writes:

[H]e would go to São Cristóvão, where Maria Inês must have remained, from time to time. He would review the old neighborhood, the familiar streets, all the witnesses of that past he wanted to bury, like a *cadaver.*

To evoke it was to reopen a hidden *sore,* to bring to consciousness all the bitterness put to rest by his recent triumphs.

At night, after the trips to São Cristóvão, the usual clique would certainly see a more stuttering, more taciturn, more susceptible little Machado. (my emphasis)[42]

The words "cadaver" and "sore" suggest infection, decay, death. This aura of unhealthiness is reinforced by the visit's negative effects on Machado, whose own illness, after renewed contact with his origins, is more pronounced. It is worth noting that her use of the diminutive form, "little Machado" (*Machadinho* in the original), is infantilizing in this context. Miguel Pereira labels Machado a "nevropata," employing a general term describing a person suffering from any disease of the nervous system (25). At other points in the text, she mentions that he suffered specifically from epilepsy and a stutter.

Miguel Pereira often couples references to Machado's *mulatice,* or other aspects of his appearance with references to his illness, referring to him variously as "o mulato feio e gago" [the ugly, stuttering mulatto] (68), "Esse homem doente e feio" [that sick and ugly man] (118), and "esse homem feio e gago" [that ugly, stuttering man] (120). Her inclusion of a racial marker in lists of his "ills," as in "epilepsy, *mulatice,* and stuttering," suggests that Machado's race is somehow connected to his health, not to mention his handsomeness (154). His *mulatice,* like his epilepsy and his stuttering, has no cure. Still, Machado must combat them to achieve greatness, and so she claims, "he fought against the impulses of the neurotics and the affectations of the mestizos—two perils that threatened him."[43] As we have seen above, Lima Barreto's race and illness are linked in a similar fashion as Miguel Pereira draws comparisons between the writers' "deficiencies" in *Prosa de ficção* and suggests that Lima Barreto, less successful than Machado at combatting his ills, died before he could fully realize his literary potential.

In *A vida de Gonçalves Dias,* Miguel Pereira also suggests a connection between the poet's race and his psychological health and portrays him as a man with an unhealthy attitude toward women. Several specific relationships are discussed including that between Gonçalves Dias and his white stepsister: "A psychoanalyst might have uncovered terrible complexes. In searching his verses, he might have caught a glimpse of revealing evidence, above all in the evocation of the sister who may have become his feminine ideal, so purely and intensely did he love her in his arid childhood."[44] Miguel Pereira distances herself somewhat from the conjecture that the author may have suffered from "terrible complexes" by inserting the imaginary figure of a psychoanalyst between herself and the suggestion. But she goes on to speak directly to his treatment of women in general: "Gonçalves

Dias spent his life taking revenge on women—taking revenge on their bodies for the affection, the understanding, he failed to find in their hearts."[45] In her reading, he lived in search of an ideal love which, by definition, he was unable to realize.

Ascribing his inappropriate behavior to a possible childhood complex centered around the taboo of incest—which, it should be emphasized, she bases entirely upon her reading of the poems he wrote about his stepsister— Miguel Pereira also suggests that Gonçalves Dias suffered from the "painful instability" of men of mixed race (110). At another point in the biography, while discussing his unduly harsh treatment of his wife, she reminds the reader that the author's equilibrium was never perfect or stable and that his overreactions were a consequence of his "psychic imbalance" (305). For Miguel Pereira, the "imbalance," "instability," or "disequilibrium" suffered by Gonçalves Dias does not always affect his behavior. He is not described as unstable, for example, as he patiently waits to become a nationally known writer: "He awaited his hour tranquilly, without of shadow of intellectual *mulatice*."[46] *Mulatice* in this context is clearly assigned a negative meaning as it is set in opposition to "tranquilly." Gonçalves Dias seems only to suffer *mulatice* where women are concerned.

The two biographies and *Prosa de ficção* reveal that Miguel Pereira appears to foreground race in her critical writing while often privileging other (usually economic/class) influences on her subjects. This *e-racing* combined with a focus on work as the cure for poverty and the means to social ascension situates her writing within the Brazilian nationalist discourse of the 1930s. While she does at times make obvious and general racist statements such as "[b]etween the white masters and the black slaves were the Amerindians and the mestizos, who chose to live in indolence and laziness," her individual treatment of the authors she studies moves her away from such explanations.[47] As with her discussion of Gonçalves Dias's psychological "complex," Miguel Pereira's psychoanalysis in the biographies is based largely upon readings of poetry and fiction. *A vida de Gonçalves Dias* and, to an even greater extent, *Machado de Assis* are interpretations of the authors' creative writings that support Miguel Pereira's assumptions about their personalities. She is, in effect, psychoanalyzing the "founding fathers" of Brazilian literature, strongly suggesting that what makes these writers psychologically "unwell" or "imbalanced" is their mixed race. She calls attention to their mixed race not to affirm it, but to point to it as a barrier to success. Machado de Assis, Gonçalves Dias, and Lima Barreto are successful writers to the extent that they are able to overcome their negatively defined *mulatice*. Yet Miguel Pereira's writings also suggest that *mulatice* or "mestiçagem" is precisely what makes these authors truly Brazilian, especially Gonçalves Dias, whom she holds up as a product of Brazil's three founding races: "The greatest importance is still attributed to the blood—or the bloods—that she [his mother] transmitted to the poet. All of those who wrote about Gonçalves Dias, from Sílvio Romero and José Veríssimo until today, are unanimous in proclaiming that his temperament is explained by the combined inheritance of the three races—the Portuguese from the father, the Indian and the Black from the mother."[48] In this racialized assessment of Gonçalves Dias's character, Miguel Pereira expresses no disagreement with her predecessors.

This paradoxical treatment of race is a product of the ways in which intellectuals like Miguel Pereira were thinking about racial issues in Brazil at the time. In his essay "Racial Ideas and Social Policy in Brazil, 1870–1940," Thomas Skidmore traces how the Brazilian elite of the period responded to the challenge of keeping up with European "scientific racism" while forging a sense of Brazilian identity which accounted for their racially mixed society. The compromise they reached is what he refers to as the "whitening ideal." Though they accepted the concept of a hierarchy of civilizations that placed the white European at the top, because of Brazil's racial heterogeneity, they could not fully accept racist determinism. Their nation would be forever doomed to inferiority. Instead, they ignored the insistence of European scientific racists that racial mixture led to degeneration and looked for ways to "whiten" the population and thus eventually move Brazilian civilization to a "higher" level. Officially, this led to such measures as the encouragement of immigration from Europe and restrictions on the immigration of Blacks.

With the publication in 1933 of Gilberto Freyre's *Casa grande e senzala* [translated as *The Masters and the Slaves*], Brazilian intellectuals found support for their rejection of the mixed-race degeneracy argument. Freyre was a student of the anthropologist Franz Boas, a well-known proponent of cultural versus racial explanations for human behavioral differences. In *Casa grande e senzala*, a social history of the slave plantations of Northeastern Brazil in the sixteenth and seventeenth centuries, Freyre argues that the history of racial mixture has led to the creation of the nation's unique culture. Freyre's emphasis on the contributions of non-whites to Brazilian culture in *Casa grande e senzala* and its continuation, *Sobrados e mucambos* [translated as *The Mansions and the Shanties*], which covers the eighteenth and nineteenth centuries, could have suggested that the races be seen as equal in potential and in their value to Brazilian society. As Skidmore notes, the actual effect of Freyre's studies was not to promote racial equality. They served instead to reinforce the whitening ideal by demonstrating that a dominant white elite had picked up useful cultural traits from its close contact with subordinate Afro-Brazilians and Amerindians (22). Though Freyre's work embodied a valorization of the African and the Amerindian, the Portuguese (white European) element took precedence in his portrayal. Through this process, Brazil's mixed-race population became an idealized group owing to the super-adaptability of its white component.[49]

By the time Lúcia Miguel Pereira began to pubish her literary criticism, the nineteenth-century myth of Brazil's three founding races was no longer problematic. For, as she notes in her analysis of Graça Aranha's novel *Canaã* (1902), attitudes about race had changed due to Freyre's work. In Aranha's time, she writes, "[t]hat feeling of racial inferiority, from which only Gilberto Freyre came to free us, oppressed us all."[50] Still, as I have indicated in Miguel Pereira's literary criticism, the valorization of the mestizo does not necessarily lead to a valorization of the non-white components of his racial background.[51] What is valued and emphasized in her writings on mestizo authors is the extent to which they were able to rise socially. In effect, she details in their biographies the process by which Machado de Assis and Gonçalves Dias "whitened" themselves.[52] Her writing shows how, through their labors and simultaneous denial of their non-white heritages, they were largely successful in making themselves acceptable to the white social elites of their respective lifetimes. As they are portrayed in Miguel Pereira's writing, they worked their way into whiteness.

An emphasis on work is part of the Brazilian nationalist discourse of the 1930s and particularly of the "Estado Novo," the governmental regime extending from 1937 to 1945. Brazilian sociologist Renato Ortiz describes how Freyre's *Casa grande e senzala* facilitates the formation of the image of the ideal national subject, the "homem brasileiro," during this period:

> The book makes possible an unequivocal affirmation of a people who still debated the ambiguities of their own definition. They transform themselves into a national unit. By reworking the problematic of Brazilian culture, Gilberto Freyre offers the Brazilian an identity card. The ambiguity of the identity of the national Self forged by the nineteenth-century intellectuals could hold up no longer. It had become incompatible with the country's process of economic and social development. . . .[I]n the 30s there is an effort to radically transform the concept of the *homem brasileiro*. Qualities like "laziness" and "indolence," considered inherent to the mestizo race, are substituted by an ideology of work.[53]

Paradoxically, *Casa grande e senzala,* a study of cultural dynamics based on race, plays a role in the process by which the definition of national identity moves away from racial and cultural differentiation toward one of economic distinction. The "homem brasileiro" of the 1930s and 1940s is the "homem novo," the worker. These are years in which extensive labor legislation is enacted, a political ideology of the valorization of work is elaborated, and the role and place of the national worker is "rehabilitated" (Gomes 151).

Lúcia Miguel Pereira's critical writing reflects common Brazilian attitudes about race and nationality in the 1930s and 1940s. While race is not ignored, it is viewed through the lens of work. Mestizo authors rise socially by means of their literary efforts. During this process, they adapt to and become accepted by the Brazilian social elite. Miguel Pereira places little value on the writers' African or Amerindian cultural backgrounds. In fact, as I have argued, she seems to link their non-white characteristics with their illnesses and psychological problems. Her views on race and culture are in keeping with those of "anti-racists" of the early twentieth century like Franz Boas and Gilberto Freyre. Though they did not consider the races unequal in potential, they did believe in a hierarchy of cultures. For Boas, all cultures shared common values, and those values were most apparent in European culture: "[H]is basic defense of primitive peoples implied a hierarchy since his invariable point in comparing cultures was that each could potentially achieve the highest culture, which was always Europe's" (Degler *Search* 80). Lúcia Miguel Pereira's argument for a "relativist" approach to literary criticism, one that somehow takes into account the "incipient nature" of Brazilian literature, indicates that she ascribes to the same hierarchical belief.

By positing European literature as a norm, Miguel Pereira sets for Brazilian literature the impossible task of achieving an ideal it can never attain: the simultaneous goals of distinguishing Brazilian culture from European culture and making Brazilian culture emulate European culture are mutually exclusive. Because she does not recognize that holding European literature as an ideal is incompatible with distinguishing a non-European national literature, Lúcia Miguel Pereira, like other Brazilian intellectuals looking to Europe as a model, must somehow compensate for her country's mixed-race population. The move from race-based to culture-based explanations of human behavior (as exemplified in the work of Gilberto Freyre) provides her a solution. A belief in a hierarchy of cultures allows for the supervaluation of European culture without denying *potential* equality to all cultures. Behind the "whitening" pursued by Miguel Pereira and her contemporaries is a desire for Brazilian society to progress toward the European, the white, the healthy, the normal, the superior culture.

We can detect this whitening tendency in Miguel Pereira's criticism of Machado de Assis and Gonçalves Dias. As she rewrites their lives, she moves them toward her ideal. In the closing pages of *Machado de Assis,* she imagines Machado's thoughts on his deathbed: "he must have felt the difference between the *little mulatto* born nearly seventy years earlier in the hovel in Livramento and the *writer* who would die enveloped in respect" (my emphasis).[54] Through the biography, Miguel Pereira has shown us that difference that Machado must have felt. She has transformed him from a little mulatto boy into a writer.

Gonçalves Dias undergoes a similar transformation though Miguel Pereira's racial portrait of him is more complex. In the beginning pages of the biography, she agrees with her predecessors that Gonçalves Dias's temperament is the result of his mixed race. Later she writes: "Actually, Gonçalves Dias was more Brazilian, in inspiration, in sensibility and in form than all the poets who preceded him; what we do not know is if he would not have been so had he been only mulatto, or *cafuzo* or even white."[55] Was Gonçalves Dias the "most Brazilian" of poets because of his mixed race? She follows the question with a brief discussion of racial versus cultural explanations:

> The very temperament and the environment in which he lived themselves could have made him permeable to our things. One could object that his temperament was the fruit of the three bloods that ran in his veins. There is no doubt about that. But how to distinguish that which came from the white, or the Indian, or the Black? At the same time it's not difficult to know what he received from his era and the conditions of his life.[56]

Miguel Pereira opts for a cultural explanation without rejecting the racial inheritance element entirely—it is simply impossible to verify. She goes on to suggest that an interest in the racial origins of Brazil could have awakened in "any poet who had been born with Independence and had begun to write when the Empire had scarcely begun to solidify itself in a moment of intense nationalism."[57] This argument for culture would ring more true if her biographical study actually described the socio-cultural context in which Gonçalves Dias lived, what he received from his epoch. The allusion she makes to a period of "intense nationalism" is one of very few socio-historical references in the book. Despite her move toward a cultural explanation, the passage above reveals that Miguel Pereira has not escaped an us/them dichotomy—he was permeable to *our things*—that surely has a racial base.

What ultimately prevents Miguel Pereira from analyzing the cultural context in both of the biographies is her relentless psychoanalytical focus. Through an understanding of the minds of these men, we are meant to better understand their works and vice versa. The result is narrowly focused biography in which sections of novels and poems are reproduced as if they were spoken in the voice of the author himself. With this technique, Miguel Pereira creates a kind of closed circuit in which there is little room for outside influences—we read her reading of the author's mind. Her psychological diagnoses tend to suggest that the authors' "deficiencies" or neuroses stem from their racial backgrounds. Despite her stated belief in cultural versus racial explanations and her appeal to a historically based relative approach to literature, Miguel Pereira's criticism—particularly the literary biographies—rests in part on her assumptions about race and psychology rather than about history or culture.

Although she never really tells us how Gonçalves Dias was a product of his time, Miguel Pereira's assertion that "qualquer poeta" could have developed his interests indicates a desire to move away from a race-based interpretation of his life and work. But her claim that Gonçalves Dias's poetry is more Brazilian than that of all of his predecessors makes a complete avoidance of race impossible. Being truly Brazilian during the nineteenth century meant being concerned with the origins of the nation, and ideas about Brazil's origins were informed by the myth of the three founding races. Though this myth had lost its power by the time Lúcia Miguel Pereira wrote her criticism, the impetus to define a Brazilian national literature had not. Each of Miguel Pereira's major critical writings engages in the discourse of the nation. Her two literary biographies treat the men she considers to be "our first great poet" and "our greatest novelist." And her argument for a historically relative critical approach which opens *Prosa de ficção: de 1870 a 1920* is based on her view of the Brazilian nation as "a young people."

In tracing Miguel Pereira's criticism we have moved from the problem of the silent issue of gender to its potential site of displacement—race. The issue of race in her work leads us to discussions of class and illness and their constraints upon social mobility. All of this is embedded in her discourse on national identity which forms the central concern of her critical works. If my reading of Lúcia Miguel Pereira's literary criticism leads away from discussions of gender, this is due to the fact that her critical work does not treat issues of gender as integral to the problem of the nation. While there is room for a certain type of discussion of race within the discourse of nationalism, gender has been displaced from this discursive space.

One might ask, then, whether it is productive to study Miguel Pereira's critical works from a feminist perspective given that this leads to a seemingly endless process of deferral. It appears that we can never make her fictional work and her critical work coincide. Approaching her writing from a feminist perspective does, however, prove productive. It helps explain her peculiar silence about women writers while at the same time she highlights women's issues in her fiction. Within the cultural constraints in which she worked, issues of gender are absent from the discussions of a Brazilian nationalist identity—race and class are primary elements. As a critic, she finds none of the literature by Brazilian women engaged with the main aesthetic, cultural, and national movements of her day. In Lúcia Miguel Pereira we find an individual whose work appears, from our position, deeply conflicted and in some respects contradictory, almost incompatible.

We are left with an unsettling situation. Clearly, taken as a body of work, Miguel Pereira's writing exemplifies how a concern for women's issues and an engagement in the discourses of national culture cannot be expressed in the same medium. Women's issues, however, can be addressed in the novel. There they are confined to the private space of the home, concerned with the domestic and consumed through the privacy of individual readers engaging with the text in isolation. There is no place for women's issues in the public debate on national identity as Ortiz's phrase "homem brasileiro" suggests. In terms of literature, this debate takes place within literary criticism. Miguel Pereira's own literary works, which as we have seen are all women-centered, have no place in her definition of Brazilian literature—she herself writes women writers out of Brazilian literary history. Their inclusion is inconsistent with a national project. As Miguel Pereira's novels so clearly demonstrate, women are absent from the question of national literature because they have been displaced from considerations of the national and the public.

3

From Consumption to Production: Victoria Ocampo as Cultural Critic

The place of Victoria Ocampo within the history of Latin American cultural criticism is a contested one, and discussion of her work must take this tension into account. Ocampo's position as a critic differs so greatly from Miguel Pereira's that another critical register is required when we approach her work. Miguel Pereira does not write about her positioning as an author and a critic. Little in her criticism satisfies the biographical curiosity of a reader intrigued by this woman's apparent acceptance and success within a male-dominated discipline. Indeed, there are no biographical studies of Miguel Pereira at all, and virtually no published information about her life is available. By contrast, Victoria Ocampo foregrounded the autobiographical form as a means of literary expression. Her autobiographical "I" is as present as her critical eye, and, as has been suggested, it is Ocampo's "I" that forms the central and captivating subject of all of her written works.

Her choice of autobiographical forms has led some writers to focus critical attention primarily on biographical rather than literary or cultural issues. For example, *Sur,* the literary journal founded by Victoria Ocampo, stands as the work for which she is best known. Yet much of what is written about Ocampo ignores the journal as a literary/cultural catalyst and tends more toward treatment of her as an icon. Cristina Lisi has documented this tendency with regard to criticism of *Sur.* By Lisi's count, only four articles specifically about *Sur* were published before Ocampo's death in 1979: "If one considers the entirety of the published works, the majority are centered on Victoria Ocampo, principally on her literary *personality* and collaterally—as part of her work—the magazine is mentioned" (my emphasis).[1]

The criticism tends to sensationalize the figure of Ocampo as a celebrity, as an ingenue, with a lesser focus on her publishing career.[2]

If Ocampo's autobiographical style invites us to examine her biography, the challenge in studying her work is to accomplish this without becoming so engrossed in the details of her life and their relationship to her writing that readings from other vantage points—those that do not focus exclusively on her life story as the explanation for the type of writing she does—are obscured. Nevertheless, to ignore the autobiographical aspect of her writing is not possible. Ocampo constantly inserts her self as subject into her texts. It is productive to consider her writing not only in terms of her gender position—a central concern for her within the autobiographical framework that has subsequently been the focus of most of the critical studies of her work—but also from other points of view. Ocampo's writings have not been well contextualized historically, perhaps because of the personal focus assumed by most critical studies. A broader approach might consider her class position and place her within a Latin American context while maintaining a focus on issues of gender. At the least, a more inclusive reading may allow us to understand her strategy of publicizing the personal as an attempt to transform the meaning of the public.

Ocampo's public stature challenges the stereotype of Latin American women's writing as private: "In this sense the attitude of the male autobiographer and that of the female do not differ greatly and the cliché of a certain 'feminine writing,' composed entirely of interiors and distant from history, becomes relative: applicable not to every woman who writes but rather to those (the majority) whose public representation is reduced, not assumed, or not recognized."[3] Ironically, then, because her approach to autobiography is not distinct from a masculine autobiographical discourse, Ocampo's writings do not represent the gender stereotype. Neither, as I shall argue, is Ocampo's literary criticism interiorized and divorced from historical context despite its personal tone. Though her writings challenge the public/private binary, Ocampo's work has been located within the realm of the private and, as such, devalued. Furthermore, autobiography itself, as Sylvia Molloy contends, has not been a valued form in Latin American writing:

for not corresponding to supposed models of the genre (take for example nineteenth-century European autobiographical contexts), Spanish American autobiography is disdained as a hybrid without recognition that that very hybridity is what makes it distinctive. As such, Spanish American autobiography has come to perform a thankless function: that of subaltern text, source of data for literary history, appendix of the work of an author, but lacking its own value.[4]

Under such conditions, Ocampo's writing seemingly invites multiple marginalization as the product of a woman writer, employing what in Latin America is traditionally considered an inferior, hybrid form.

Yet I will argue that her writing constitutes a resistance to erasure, to being locked out of established literary institutions. Though her "personal" approach is read as unconventional in traditional literary criticism, Ocampo clearly seeks a role in literary history and national history through the recording of her observations.[5] In several instances she suggests that the merit of her approach lies in its deliberate subjectivity: "when I have proposed to describe a person who has nothing to do with my circumstance, when I have wanted to limit myself to an *objective* analysis, I have quickly realized that I was referring to a being I had never seen as if it were part of my intimate life." She goes on to ask, "Is there another way to deeply understand a person? If it exists, I have never come upon it. When my *Testimonios* reach a level of *High Fidelity* it is because they take that route."[6] This represents more than a simple rationalization of her writing style after the fact. Ocampo's approach reflects a belief on her part that one's "self" is always inextricable from one's "object" of study.

Though Ocampo's self-representation is tied to her nation's culture, her project differs from that of her male predecessors in that her desire to be "objective" through her subjectivity is linked to her desire to write "like a woman":

> My only ambition is to some day write, more or less well, more or less poorly, but like a woman. If the image of Aladdin were to possess a magic lamp, and through it I were given the writing style of a Shakespeare, a Dante, a Goethe, a Cervantes, a Dostoevsky, I really would not take advantage of the deal. For I understand that a woman can't relieve herself of her feelings and thoughts in a masculine style, in the same way that she can't speak with a man's voice.[7]

Ocampo was not interested in an "objective" stance that would deny or efface her sex. Her intention to write "like a woman" causes critics to view her writing as the working out of personal demons. I would like to consider this desire for representation as something more than private therapy. For example, Ocampo's search for other authors' self-representations in their writings may be viewed as an attempt to forge literary links. By connecting her life/writing with that of foreign authors she draws not only herself but Argentina, by extension, into the international literary establishment. After all, Ocampo considers herself to be quintessentially Argentine, and the connection between herself and her nation (or even herself *as* her nation) is one that is frequently stressed in her writing. As Francine Masiello notes, Ocampo often reads her own body as a forming nation, making an explicit connection between herself and Argentina. In so doing, "she forges an alternative female autobiography in which the individual determines national destiny" (*Between* 164). Such a claim to representation is not entirely circumscribed by what is conventionally understood as the private.

Extending herself beyond Argentina, Ocampo at times suggests that her situation is "essentially" American. In the essay "Palabras francesas," she explores the implications and difficulties surrounding her use of French as a primary language. The closing paragraphs indicate the extent to which the author identifies her struggles with those of "America":

> What I conclude from my reflections about this subject is that none of this would have happened if I had not been American. If I had not been essentially American I would not have spoken an impoverished overseas Spanish. . . . If I had not been American, finally, neither would I likely feel this thirst for explaining, for explaining us and for explaining myself. In Europe when something is produced, one would say that it is explained in advance. . . . So, here we are obliged to close our eyes and advance painfully, gropingly, toward ourselves; looking for the way in which old explanations can be accommodated to new problems. We vacillate, we stumble, we fool ourselves, we tremble, but we continue obstinate. Though the results obtained may be mediocre for the moment, what does it matter?[8]

While talking about "America" and "Americans," Ocampo simultaneously talks about herself. There is a fluidity between identities. The language she employs here evokes descriptions elsewhere of her struggles for self-knowledge and self-expression. She makes explicit the links between her personal efforts and those of Americans when she goes on in the same essay to say, "I've said before that I do not take myself for a writer, I'm totally ignorant about the occupation. I am a simple human being in search of expression."[9]

Not surprisingly, Ocampo's claims to represent Argentines and other Americans have led to charges of elitism, another reason for which her writing is often dismissed. These charges are bolstered by characterizations of her work as being directed to an exclusive group. Her subject matter (and her social life) places Ocampo within a restricted international cultural elite. By claiming the power of representation, representation of both self and nation, she claims a position of power. Similarly, her connection to a cultural elite is a manifestation of economic and cultural capital. Yet, despite her privileged class position, her direct access to this facet of cultural power is blocked by the fact that she is a woman.

Cultural analyses based primarily on questions of social class have recently come under scrutiny from feminists disappointed in the lack of attention to all women's issues. I will argue that Ocampo's writing, and particularly her feminist writing, should not be dismissed on the basis of her class interests. While not losing sight of the fact that Ocampo's life and writing differ from those of less privileged women, I agree with Carolyn Heilbrun that "sneering at privileged women, whether or not they recognize their difference in experience from working class women, has done nothing to aid the cause of feminism" (64). While Ocampo may have been blind to certain issues, she wrote consistently about women's concerns and about particular (albeit elite) women writers. As contemporary critics continue to grapple with the complex intersections of gender, class, and race, it is unreasonable to devalue Ocampo's writing for revealing them. Recent critical studies focus on the conflicted nature of Ocampo's views, carving out something of a middle ground in the criticism.[10] Unfortunately, when conflict becomes the subject of criticism in Ocampo's case, the temptation is to set up inescapable binary schemes in which her feminism and her class position seem somehow to cancel each other out.

What is needed is a means of dealing with writing which is at times both feminist and elitist. Though I will be referring to several critical pieces throughout this discussion, it should be emphasized that (as Lisi documents) relatively little has been written about Ocampo's actual writing. I do not argue in favor of ignoring the implications of Ocampo's elitism, but would suggest instead that we not ignore her writing because of it. In considering Ocampo's work, I will focus on its transgressive nature as a social act, viewing it as a challenge rather than a reaction to the conventions of literary authority. In particular, I will explore the power of Ocampo's personal stance to draw attention to and expose the myth of objectivity employed in masculinist literary critical discourse.

To achieve this, the first part of my discussion examines some of the issues and problems raised by readers of Ocampo's texts. An overview of her various critical writings with special attention to her ten volumes of *Testimonios,* the books that contain most of her literary critical essays, follows. The discussion concludes with a close analysis of two of Ocampo's critical essays. My goal is to evaluate Ocampo's choice of autobiography as a literary critical tool while avoiding an approach which focuses exclusively on gender. As such, I hope to locate Ocampo's writing within a broader cultural framework.

Though she received an education considered appropriate to her social position and sex, Victoria Ocampo referred to herself as an autodidact. In a speech delivered to the Sociedad Argentina de Escritores in 1950 titled "Malandanzas de una autodidacta,"[11] she describes "what was considered convenient to teach the women of my class," noting first, "I imagine that in the poor classes teaching must be nil": "grammar (read orthography), some elementary math, a lot of catechism, sacred history, a smattering of universal history, another smattering of Argentine history, some vague notions about natural sciences, languages (especially French or English) . . . piano."[12] Her use of the term "convenient" is indicative of the resentment Ocampo felt over what she perceived to be the inadequacies of her formal education. The gaps in and peculiarities of her training and its consequences for her later intellectual development are a theme that recurs throughout Ocampo's writing, "Malandanzas de una autodidacta" being one of several instances in which she laments what she believes to be her educational disadvantage.

The second volume of her autobiography makes clear the details of the repressive though luxurious environment in which the author was raised. In letters she wrote to Delfina Bunge as a teenager which she includes in this volume subtitled "El imperio insular," Ocampo expresses her feelings of imprisonment, loneliness, and anger at sexual double standards (79–139). Commenting on the letters and this period in her life, she writes: "My point of view was that of a capable adolescent who can neither take advantage of nor fully develop her talents by means of an adequate education, *and who intuits this daily.*"[13] In addition to limiting the range of her formal studies, Ocampo's family and tutors also censored her reading material until she reached adulthood: "The discovery of Wilde's *De Profundis* under my pillow achieved the proportions of a catastrophe. The book was confiscated by the household censorship without my understanding the motive, which made me more indignant. I was, after all, fully nineteen years old at the time."[14] In defiance of their restrictions, Ocampo read avidly, both to compensate for the education she felt she was deprived of and as a means of escape.

From the outset, then, literature played a central role in Victoria Ocampo's intellectual and emotional development. When the Ocampos forbade their daughter to pursue a career in the theater, which she later described as "what seemed to be my true vocation" (*Testimonios* 5 18), she settled for a career involving literature. Her choice of vocation was not without its difficulties, however, for as Ocampo later noted in her autobiography, a literary career (or any career, for that matter) was not considered suitable for Argentine women of her class.

In terms of her academic training, Ocampo learned that having been taught to read and write primarily in French proved to be an obstacle when she found herself having to translate her own work into Spanish: "And I could not escape this process given that my principle wish was to direct myself to my compatriots."[15] It was due to the social standing of Ocampo's family that her formal education included more French and English than Spanish. The fact that she wrote in French has been taken by some as a sign of her elitism and offered as proof that she was not "genuinely Argentine." Some critics, including Max Daireaux in his *Panorama de la Littérature Hispano-Américaine,* have taken Ocampo's writing in French as a sign of her coquetry.[16] Others have noted her struggle to express herself in Spanish and understood it as yet another element of her "anxiety" about writing. Ocampo's use of the term "compatriots" reminds us that she did indeed concern herself with an Argentine national audience for her writing.

While most of her critics explore the significance of the fact that Ocampo wrote primarily in French, little attention is paid to what she actually did with her language skills. As Beatriz Sarlo so astutely notes, rather than use them solely for consumption, the purpose for which she was taught them, Ocampo employs her language skills for (literary) production:

> Foreign language, in women of Ocampo's background, was used to write letters, read novelettes, recite a little or attend theater productions, speak with shopkeepers or dressmakers, go to the hairdresser. Foreign language was a language of feminine consumption, not of production.
>
> Victoria Ocampo subverts it, making it productive language: to read, to receive, but also to cite, to give back. Foreign languages are not only a means of material or symbolic consumption but also, in the case of Victoria Ocampo, they are means of production.[17]

Sarlo's comments bring to mind not only Ocampo's own writing, which is often intertextual and contains numerous references to French, Italian, and English literature which she read in their original languages, but also to her work as a translator. Ocampo translated much of her own literary critical writing in order to make it available to a Spanish-reading audience. She also translated and published works by William Faulkner, Graham Greene, John Osborne, Albert Camus, and Dylan Thomas among others.[18]

One can take a step further Sarlo's notion of Ocampo using her language skills to produce rather than consume, making it a frame for the consideration of all of Ocampo's writings. She takes advantage of what her parents have given her—an elite, though limited, education and material wealth—and uses it for purposes for which it was not intended: "What her social milieu thought of as adornment, Victoria Ocampo converts into an instrument."[19] Ocampo established and funded her own literary career. In doing so, she transgressed by putting her private education to public use.

As Molloy's *At Face Value* illustrates, Ocampo had to learn new ways of reading and relating to the canon because, due to her gender, she had limited access to it (57). Ocampo's approach to literature is one that combines the read and the lived, what she calls *lo vivido* and *lo leído*. Her methods offend critics who require the separation of those spheres and who would argue for the superiority of an "objective" over a "personal" stance. As the reception of Ocampo's *De Francesca a Beatrice* attests, such arguments provide a convenient tool for excluding women en masse from the field of literary criticism.

Ocampo's first book, *De Francesca a Beatrice,* was published in Spain in 1924. She calls it a "guide book" to *The Divine Comedy* for the lay reader: "These two words are directed neither at Danteans nor at the learned, for I can teach them nothing. They are directed at common readers, those who could love this great and beautiful book and who, for one reason or another, have yet to approach it. They are directed, above all, to those who have leafed through it lazily."[20] This and other statements in the introduction suggest that Ocampo is addressing a general reading audience of which she considers herself a (not lazy) member. Still, she does not ignore the critics who have come before her: "When approaching Dante, by whatever path, one suddently runs into a numerous and terrible guard: the commentators."[21] As will often be the case with Ocampo's prefaces, her deference may be interpreted as acknowledgment of her lack of "erudition," a kind of preliminary request for forgiveness. Yet there is a deliberate tone to her remarks which cannot be ascribed solely to ignorance or to humility, for she goes on to critique her predecessors: "Bristling with erudition, they stand erect in aggressive pose over the threshold of each canto of the Poem; and their interpretations—which often contradict one another—brandished like swords, make the fearful reader back away *là dove il sol tace.*"[22] In her rebuke, Ocampo suggests that her own reading will be more intelligible and perhaps more useful to the reader, like a "Baedeker" of the *Divine Comedy* (*Testimonios* 5 23).

De Francesca a Beatrice is a relatively short book, and Ocampo makes no claims to offering an exhaustive reading. Instead, she highlights what most interests her in sections named for Dante's titles "El Infierno," "El Purgatorio," and "El Paraíso," at times skipping huge portions of the poem and at others lingering over a particular section. As the title suggests, her book focuses on the female figures of Francesca and Beatrice. Initiating what I have noted is a trend in analyses of her work, critics at that time read Ocampo's longstanding affair with her husband's cousin into her interest in Francesca, the adulteress.[23]

De Francesca a Beatrice was not well received by critics. Ocampo showed a portion of the manuscript to Paul Groussac, Director of the National Library, whose negative comments she summarizes in "Malandanzas de una autodidacta." Groussac tells her,

> one shouldn't write about the *Divine Comedy* if one doesn't have new information or interpretations. Apparently this is not your case. You know French, but it isn't your language. Why don't you write in Spanish? (Curious advice coming from whom it came. "And you?" I might have asked in reply [Groussac was French].) Why, furthermore, don't you choose another less Dantesque, not to say pedantic, type of subject if you really feel you must write? For example, personal experiences lived by you, etc.[24]

Ocampo responded that she felt her reading of Dante was a personal experience. (We might ask a converse question raised by Groussac's statements: why is Dante a more appropriate theme for a man?) Ocampo's friend, Angel de Estrada, also read the manuscript and was slightly more detailed in his critique. He found her style "overly personal, *completely direct*" and likened this literary exposure to the inappropriateness (in an earlier time) of women showing their bodies in public (qtd. in Ocampo, *Autobiografía 3* 106). As Delfina Muschietti notes, even a "positive" review from Brandán Caraffa displays the limitations and powerlessness attached to the "feminine": "Victoria Ocampo is a writer by nature . . . And such an enchanting posture of humility hers is. She opens the locked door of eternal desperation with such a feminine gesture."[25] These preliminary critics reveal obstacles with which Ocampo will have to reckon throughout her writing career as she continues to develop her critical voice: the question of language (what does it mean to write in French or Spanish?); the debate over appropriate themes for women's writing, and the closely related issue of the correct style for literary criticism.

A debate with another critic, José Ortega y Gasset, reveals Ocampo's continued engagement with these questions. Ortega y Gasset's press, Revista de Occidente, published the first edition of *De Francesca a Beatrice* in 1924. In the epilogue that he appended to the book, Ortega y Gasset simultaneously praises Ocampo for her ideally feminine qualities—"You, Madam, are an exemplary apparition of femininity"—and prescribes women's role in the cultural world as that of perfection-inspiring muse.[26] He argues that women are meant to be passive feelers, not thinkers: "Woman's strength is not knowing but rather feeling. To know things is to have their concepts and definitions and this is man's work."[27] Literary criticism, in Ortega y Gasset's version of the theory of separate spheres, is not for women. Apparently Ocampo had no control over the production of her book since she clearly disagrees with the statements made in the epilogue. She responds in an essay titled "Contestación a un epílogo de Ortega y Gasset" in which she refutes the passivity ascribed by him: "I must confess that I have read Dante with love, simply, and that I have read him actively, not passively."[28]

Ocampo and Ortega y Gasset continued their disagreement on the role of women in literature through essays published over several decades. For example, when Ortega y Gasset publishes an article in his *Revista de Occidente* praising Anna de Noailles as an exceptional woman writer—"there may not have been, in all of modern literatures, another woman gifted with the same poetic impetus"—Ocampo responds by arguing against the idea of "exceptional" women and against the notion of separate spheres.[29] She points out that Ortega y Gasset undermines his praise of Noailles by openly questioning women's poetic ability in general: "He doesn't disguise for us that in his conception of woman, lyric genius has no place."[30] To Ortega y Gasset's suggestion that if women must write, they should stick to letters, Ocampo responds: "If Ortega considers that only the epistolary genre reconciles with femininity, it is—and he proclaims it so—because the letter is directed at only one being, not at everyone, and because, as opposed to man, woman is made for intimacy."[31] She disagrees, arguing that letters are not necessarily written with a one-person audience in mind: "Does Ortega perchance suppose that the letters of Marie de Rabutin-Chantal about the wedding of Mademoiselle or the death of Turena were edited with less attention to the public that the poems of Anna de Noailles or the novels of Virginia Woolf?"[32] Ortega y Gasset's logic of separate spheres is flawed for

Ocampo: "According to Ortega, man and woman cannot achieve their maximum expansion outside of two separate spheres. For man, public life; for woman, private life."[33] She wonders how men and women would ever truly communicate, locked as they would be in their prescribed locations. Furthermore, in the area of literature, the distinction man=public, woman= private is false, not only because women write well outside of letters (which are not necessarily private), but because Ocampo considers all writing to be personal:

> I believe that all writers of breeding, whatever their sex or their mode of expression may be, write foremost for themselves, to free themselves of themselves, to arrive at a clarification of themselves, to communicate with themselves. For only one who has already communicated with oneself communicates with others. And what is that *public* Ortega talks about? No more than a few people.[34]

In these comments we hear echoes of Ocampo's assertion that the author is always within the text, whatever the genre, and regardless of whether or not he or she calls attention to that fact. She elaborates on her thoughts about the sexes and the genres many years later in an essay on the letters of Gabriela Mistral. Referring back to the debate with Ortega y Gasset, she suggests that the real distinction between public and private in terms of letter writing has to do with whether or not the writer, male or female, writes "with an eye to posterity" (*Testimonios* 6 63).

The debate with Ortega y Gasset offers several insights into readings of Ocampo's literary criticism. Though some of her comments may suggest that she placed criticism beneath fiction or poetry in a hierarchy of literary genres, she clearly wrote her "testimonial" or "personal" criticism "with an eye to posterity."[35] Beginning with the publication of *De Francesca a Beatrice,* Ocampo's work elicits paternalistic criticism like Ortega y Gasset's that attempts to devalue her writing. That such criticism has been successful in its aims is evident in the way in which Ocampo's writing is presently defined. One contemporary example is the omission of Ocampo's *Testimonios* from the bibliography of "collected essays of criticism" in *Argentine Literature: A Research Guide* (Foster). The guide lists eight books by Ocampo's Argentine contemporary, the literary critic Roberto F. Giusti, including his memoirs, *Visto y vivido: anécdotas, semblanzas, confesiones y batallas.* Yet, unlike Ocampo, Giusti renounces any historical aims for this text: "[I]t does not occur to the author to offer himself as a historical source. He only aspires that his disperse recollections be read with the pleasure that one can read a collection of anecdotes and depictions from life and the consequent marginal reflections."[36] Giusti apparently does not consider this particular book literary criticism, though it appears in the bibliography.

There are more similarities between Ocampo's literary criticism and that of her Argentine contemporaries than one would imagine after reading her critics. Giusti, like Ocampo, published his literary memoirs. And in his *Literatura y vida* (1939), also categorized in the research guide as literary criticism, he includes five essays that were originally speeches. The rest are reprints of essays first published in either *La Prensa* or *Nosotros* (Giusti *Literatura* 377). Ocampo is not alone, then, in publishing collections of essays, some of which were printed elsewhere (in her case, usually in *Sur*), or in publishing speeches. And as his title suggests, Giusti's essays are not restricted to literary themes. In fact, in the opening essay of *Literatura y vida,* "Sinfonía de Buenos Aires," he narrates a historical walking tour. Divided into sections titled "En la torre y en la calle," "El descubrimiento de Buenos Aires," "El río por donde entraron los fundadores," "El Puerto por donde se entra a la colmena," "La ciudad de hoy, la ciudad de ayer," and "Diálogo de la pirámide y el obelisco," the piece makes scant reference to literature.

When he does focus on literature, Giusti takes more of a historical view than Ocampo as evidenced by his tendency to chronologize and group. His style, like hers, is often hybrid, as it is in his essay "Alfonsina Storni" (*Literatura* 97–133). Read at the Colegio Libre de Estudios Superiores after Storni's death, the essay combines personal recollections of the poet, close readings of several poems, an "examination of her poetic evolution," and a discussion of "feminine poetry," even including a brief history of women poets.

I characterize Giusti's criticism briefly here to suggest that, though Ocampo's style is generally more personal and less historical than that of her male contemporary, it is certainly not an aberration. If anything, it is Ocampo's feminism as opposed to her writing style that most differentiates her criticism. Indeed, the devaluation her work has suffered has more to do with her person than with her writing itself. Ocampo's choice of form and style, of course, affect the reception of her work since both the essay and autobiography are hazily defined and devalued genres. It is highly possible that the lack of attention to Ocampo's literary criticism also stems from a tendency to consider criticism (or anything) written by women, regardless of its style, as not being of general interest.

The relegation of Ocampo's writings to the margins of literary critical discourse is a process that begins with the publication of *De Francesca a Beatrice* and continues with her other works. Considering the sheer volume of her writing in print, it is striking how little has been published about it and in particular, about her ten volumes of *Testimonios*. As Lisi's article suggests, much of what has appeared, even what has been written about *Sur*, considered by many to be Ocampo's greatest literary accomplishment, has been about Victoria Ocampo. Be they detractors or admirers, before Ocampo's death, most critics were unable to assess *Sur*, the magazine, without assessing Victoria Ocampo, the person. Though it is possible that Ocampo's personality and physical presence were so powerful and legendary that while she was alive critics could not avert their focus from the person, it is likely that the nature of most of the critiques was simply due to the unsettling fact that Ocampo was a woman. That she employed an autobiographical style only made such criticism seem more justifiable. The resulting assessments, like Ortega y Gasset's, objectified Victoria Ocampo as woman and failed to read her deliberate use of the personal as an attempt to transform the meaning of the public.

Even after Ocampo's death, many critics do not escape the tendency to judge the person rather than the writing. In *Sur: a study of the Argentine literary journal and its role in the literary development of a culture, 1931–1970*, John King acknowledges Ocampo's activities regarding the journal but pays very little attention to her as a writer despite the fact that Ocampo was *Sur*'s most frequent contributor.[37] The first paragraph of his book indicates where he places Ocampo vis-à-vis the magazine: "Most magazines lasted only a few years or, in some cases, a few issues, but *Sur*, thanks to the quality of its contributors and the sound financial base of its founder, Victoria Ocampo, was to have an important influence on several generations" (King 1). She is seen primarily as the financial backer of the project and given credit for neither her editorial choices nor her own writings in the journal.

Though he discusses other ideological questions raised in the journal, King pays scant attention to Ocampo's feminism. Aside from her own work, there has been virtually no analysis of what Janet Greenberg calls the "steady but quiet discussions" which champion women's equality in the pages of *Sur*. Even so, as studies such as Marifran Carlson's *¡Feminismo!: The Woman's Movement in Argentina From its Beginnings to Eva Perón*, Francesca Miller's *Latin American Women and the Search for Social Justice*, and Asunción Lavrin's *Women, Feminism, and Social Change in Argentina, Chile, and Uruguay, 1890–1940* demonstrate, there is interest among Latin Americanists in examining the wide range of feminist organizations active in Latin America from the early twentieth century to the present. Ocampo herself was one of the founders of the *Unión Argentina de Mujeres*. The union, which offered social and legal services for women, was founded primarily to campaign against regressive changes in the Civil Code proposed during the administration of President Agustín P. Justo (1932–1938) (Carlson 177).

Yet in relation to Ocampo's writing, little mention is made of feminism. This lack of attention may in part be attributed to her own editorial approach. She prided herself on publishing opinions in opposition to her own, and, as Greenberg attests, her feminist ideas were marginalized in *Sur* ("Divided" 299). Indeed, her feminism would always be contradictory to her goal for the magazine to maintain a separation of the arts and politics: "In the literary domain, *Sur* placed the quality of the writer above all else whatever his or her tendencies. Letters have nothing to do with universal suffrage, or with democracy, or with Christian charity: either something has value or it doesn't."[38] Despite her claims that *Sur* is apolitical, the tension generated by Ocampo's feminism is nonetheless played out in the pages of the magazine.

In 1937, *Sur* published an exchange between Ocampo and José Bergamín consisting of an explanatory insert (presumably) written by Ocampo, a reprint of a letter attacking Ocampo that Bergamín originally published in an unidentified Buenos Aires newspaper, and two responses by Ocampo (32: 67; 33: 103–105). In his letter, Bergamín criticizes Ocampo for what he refers to as her hospitality toward a fellow Spaniard, Gregorio Marañon, whom he considers a traitor to the Republican cause. The language of his attack is personal, sexist, and condescending. He portrays Ocampo as a snob, a frivolous coquette incapable of comprehending the gravity of the war, and likens her to "certain women" who have been fooled by "marañonesque activities" (32: 69). It is his "Spaniard's duty," he concludes, to set Ocampo straight (32: 69).

Ocampo responds by condemning violent solutions to conflict. To his assertion that she should "spit in his [Marañon's] face" (32: 69) she replies: "Precisely because I am an authentic American I do not feel the need to spit in the face of any ruined Spaniard [. . .] neither do I feel the need to kill one who does not share my opinion so as to convince him or her that I am in the right. God willing, this will always be authentic americanness and destiny will not someday take us to the dead end street of violence."[39] After positioning herself as an "authentic American," Ocampo repeats her rejection of violence, this time as a woman: "Wars or revolutions, killings, in a word, horrify me and I will never admit that they are a means of resolving problems of any kind, perhaps because we women are accustomed in times of peace and war to risk our life; but to give life not death."[40] She goes on to point out that Bergamín is fighting against the "exploitation of man by man," and to ask if he has considered the exploitation of women:

> Has it never occurred to you to think that there has existed and still exists in the world a more odious exploitation than this one: that of woman by man? I refer to the position of absolute inferiority in which women have seen themselves obliged to live for centuries and which today is beginning to change. I refer to the conditions of *nonprivileged existence* to which man has reduced them by force in all social classes. I refer to the humiliation of having been treated by mens' laws for centuries as minors, as incapable, as insane to whom true responsibility is denied.[41]

Ocampo connects her argument about the subordination of women to Bergamín's letter. Arguing that the exploitation of women is as horrible an injustice as the exploitation of the Spanish proletariat, she simultaneously exposes the sexism of Bergamín's critique. Bergamín alludes to "strange complacencies" that "for me resemble 'certain women'." Ocampo responds: "We know what that 'certain' to whom naturally he adds quotation marks means. Well then; those allusions, those latent quotation marks, that appearance of sex in the moment at which you want to make me feel your contempt are unworthy of you, José Bergamín."[42]

Portions of a second letter from Bergamín are included in a second response by Ocampo, "El proletariado de la mujer," which appears in the next issue of *Sur.* He apologizes for any offense, yet continues to use Ocampo's sex as the basis of his critique. Her truth, he says, is too literary: "'Like that which leads you to that unfortunate feminist comparison between your delicate sufferings of a private woman (without quotation marks) and those of the working proletariat. God forgive you that [. . .] delicate coquetry, Victoria Ocampo!'"[43] Drawing attention again to the sexist nature of Bergamín's opinions, Ocampo defers to Emmanuel Mounier, the director of the magazine *Espirit,* to which Bergamín was a contributor: "as to my unfortunate feminist comparision, I have just found it in the writing of E. Mounier [. . .] Bergamín shouldn't have the same reason to doubt this *gentleman* that he seems to have to doubt me" (my emphasis).[44] She then quotes from Mounier's essay "La vida privada," in which he argues that women are the true proletariat: "The impossibility, for the individual, to rise to his or her own life,—which in our view defines the proletariat even more essentially than does material misery,—is the destiny of nearly all women, rich and poor, middle class, working class and peasant."[45] Ocampo ends the exchange pessimistically with what she considers the only available response: Bergamín's view of women makes communication with him impossible.

The same impossibility of communication on women's issues appears in Ocampo's exchange with Ernesto Sábato fifteen years later. Sábato, who was a longtime and frequent contributor to *Sur,* published "Sobre la metafísica del sexo" in a 1952 edition of *Sur* containing several essays on art and gender. The essay is reminiscent of Ortega y Gasset's earlier writings on men and women and their respective "natures": "Logic is man's attribute [. . .], intuition is woman's. Man is a rational being, woman is an irrational being. Man tends to the realm of the abstract, of pure ideas, of *panlogismo.* Woman moves better in the world of the concrete, of impure ideas, of the illogical."[46] That *Sur* would publish such a misogynist piece speaks both to Ocampo's view of her role as editor and to her lonely position as a feminist amongst her peers within the magazine.

Following Jung, Sábato argues that men and women have both masculine and feminine "attributes," the male artist being the perfect example: "man's creations that are more tied to his unconscious, like poetry or art, would be the expressions of his femininity. And, strictly speaking, what is more feminine than art, even though (*or because*) it is produced by men?"[47] It is worth noting he makes no mention here of the female artist. While Sábato advocates that men develop their "feminine attributes," he argues that women's development of their "masculine attributes" has led to crisis and must be reversed: "Modern society masculinized woman, falsifying with grave psychic consequences the essence of her being [. . .] If the radical crisis of our time is to be overcome, it will require the return to a feminine woman."[48] Although according to Sábato, "*woman is humanity*" (45), modern woman is the problem rather than the solution. To rectify the situation, she must return to her "femininity" and let dynamic man save civilization by developing his female attributes and thereby "feminizing society."

Ocampo's initial response to Sábato is a letter, printed in the subsequent volume of *Sur,* in which she proposes to point out errors in, not differences of opinion about, aspects of his essay. She recalls statements from Sábato's piece that she won't be addressing (presumably so preposterous they do not merit more than mention) such as "sex, which for woman is basic, has almost no importance in the actual sexual act"[49] and from his paragraph titled "Defectos del hombre y de la mujer":

The virtue of woman is centered in her altruism for the species, in her capacity for personal sacrifice in honor of her children and of the men under her care. For this reason, her world is concrete and small, personal and vital. But from there to trifles and, what is worse to pettiness, is one step. And to ant-like egotism, to tattling, to small gossip, to visceral jealousies. Man also errs, but at least he errs making world war or a philosophical system.[50]

Leaving these remarks to condemn themselves, Ocampo moves on in the body of the letter to refute Sábato's depiction of Malraux and T. E. Lawrence and the characters in their novels as examples for his arguments about the differences between the sexes. She concludes with the suggestion: "'*Let's agree to differ* . . . ' if I can't convince you," reinforcing the uncompromising tone set at the letter's opening (211–212: 169).

Sábato responds with a letter in which he accuses Ocampo of overreacting: "In a very modest and almost invisible paragraph I put a microscopic list of defects and already you are jumping on me like a furious bacchante disposed to rip me apart alive and eat me raw. Calm yourself, Victoria. It's not a big deal."[51] He objectifies and insults Ocampo, trivializing her concerns with the suggestion that she is drunkenly overexcited. His response adds another dimension to their debate by calling attention to the differences between his style and Ocampo's: "Your letter requires some urgent clarifications given that my work is longer, less picturesque and epistolary, more abstract, and less feminine finally, than your shallow judgment, I run the risk that many would take my ideas for yours."[52] The body of his letter is a numbered list of complaints about Ocampo's response. Number five touches again on the issue of approach and authority: "As to Malraux's opinions on women, you cite that once, while speaking with him, etc. Intimate meetings, teas, meals, conversations have some value for judging the personality of a writer. But the most authentic of a novelist, what is most profound and mysteriously his, will not be heard from his lips but rather from the lips of his characters, at times from the least suspicious."[53] "Intimate meetings, teas," etc. are marked here as feminine and superficial. Ocampo's knowledge of these authors, to which she had made reference in her first letter, is trivialized. Again she is disqualified as a critic on "personal" grounds.

In her second letter to Sábato, printed in the same volume of *Sur,* Ocampo defends her style: "I have responded to your long and meretricious essay of disclosure with a little letter of rubbish. But just as your essay is not obliged to adopt the epistolary style, a letter is not obliged to seem like an essay."[54] The tone of her letter is sarcastic as she mocks Sábato's letter by responding with a numbered list of her own: "I like enumerations. They have a slightly ordered air, whatever the confusion of the goods they cover."[55] As it was with Bergamín, Ocampo's exchange with Sábato is characterized by absolute differences of opinion with regards to women. In both instances, the men attack Ocampo on the basis of her gender. Ocampo responds, but hers is a lone feminist voice in the pages of *Sur*.

The contours of Ocampo's feminism manifest themselves more clearly in her series of *Testimonios*. While many of the essays that comprise these volumes were originally published in *Sur*, the two contexts show Ocampo's work to different effects. Not surprisingly, her writings appear more consistent when grouped together. This is not to suggest that the *Testimonios* are homogeneous. In fact, they are hybrid in their form, containing letters to literary figures, speeches, short essays, and even self-interviews. In Volume 7 (251–273), for instance, Ocampo interviews herself by placing ellipses where an interviewer's questions would appear and leaving the reader to ascertain the unprinted question from her response.

The form of the *Testimonios,* their simultaneous personal and critical nature, has led critics to identify the person of their author with her writing. As we have seen, this conflation often results in criticism which objectifies and stereotypes Ocampo as a woman. Ocampo's choice of style unfortunately lends itself to this type of attack because of its personal tone, which is traditionally associated with the private realm of women's discourse and is evocative of gossip and diaries. The difficulty facing the critic is to move beyond the often paternalistic reading of her work to explore the broader possibilities and meaning of her use of the personal mode.

Recent analysis of the *Testimonios* has viewed them as the product of Ocampo's struggle to shape her identity.[56] While the *Testimonios* may be read as documents of one woman's struggle for self-expression in the male-dominated world of letters, I would suggest that they may simultaneously be read for what they actually say about literature—that is, as literary criticism. The personal quality of her writing does not make her literary critical comments meditative reflections. Rather, the emphasis upon personal experience is part of the challenge Ocampo's work presents to broadening the horizons of Latin American literary criticism. Clearly Ocampo draws a distinction between creative writing and testimony, establishing a hierarchy of literary genres in which fiction and poetry rise above literary criticism. Her ascription to such a distinction does not indicate, however, that she considers her own writing an inferior form of criticism. Neither should we.

Ocampo acknowledges and defends her deliberately subjective critical stance in her writing:

> The dislike of using the pronoun "I" in literature has always seemed to me childish prejudice. In literature as in life the use of "I" may be hateful—but only when it happens to be so. The mere use of the first

person singular is not hateful in itself. Egoism is no less hateful when it is represented by an indefinite "one" or a plural "we" . . . No work of art can be created except from a more or less sublimated or transposed "I." (*33871 T.E. 53*)[57]

Ocampo's stance on critical writing is informed by the same belief: "From the moment we write, we are condemned to be unable to speak about more than ourselves, about what we've seen with our eyes, felt with our sensibilities, understood with our intelligence. Escaping this law is impossible."[58] Anticipating later-twentieth-century debates about the uses of the personal "I" in criticism, she recognizes the subjective nature of all discourse and acknowledges her subject position. The boundaries between her self and her writing become blurred.

Subjectivity is the groundwork on which Ocampo erects all her writing. As we have seen, she often identifies herself to her reading audience both as a woman and as an American. "In this America in which everything is 'in the making,' testimonies are perhaps more necessary than in any other place. And if mine mean something it is above all because I belong to her."[59] Her remarks echo those of her nineteenth-century Argentine predecessors Sarmiento and Mitre who, as we have seen, equate their life stories with the history (his story) of their nation. Though Ocampo at times laments the lack of art in her writing, she never questions her claim to represent America, a claim which offends some of her critics for its presumption and classist overtones. And like Lúcia Miguel Pereira, Ocampo considers America immature in comparison to Europe.

Ocampo's repeated defense of her use of the first person and her explanations of her style could be read as a sign of ambivalence or hesitation about her choice to write the *Testimonios* and to write them from a "subjective" stance. Her tactics may also be read as necessary in the face of repeated negative criticism over time. Ocampo finds herself arguing with Ernesto Sábato in 1952 over virtually the same issues on which she disagreed with José Ortega y Gasset fifteen years earlier. Her male counterparts did not rush to acknowledge that women possessed the intelligence and creative capacity to produce art, nor did they easily accept her as a female critic.

Ocampo's posthumously published autobiography (1979–1984) highlights her relationship to literature and its extraordinary importance to her. It is tempting to treat the autobiography as a key to all of Ocampo's writings. It could prove distracting, though, for several reasons, not the least of which is the problem of the relationship between "truth" and autobiography. For the purposes of evaluating her criticism, why would what Ocampo writes in the autobiography necessarily be any more valid than her other writing? While it would be extremely difficult to construct a discussion of Ocampo's writings without making reference to her biography, one cannot allow the biographical to obscure other approaches to her work. In particular, I would like to set aside the idea that the *Testimonios* function as some sort of mask for the "real" or "emergent" voice of Victoria Ocampo which shows itself more clearly in her autobiography. Such an approach I think runs the risk of robbing Ocampo of her critical agency and integrity.

Janet Greenberg argues that Ocampo suffered from an "anxiety over asserting a critical voice" that makes her part of a "long tradition of women writers whose work is now being reread by feminist scholars" ("Divided" 83). To emphasize Ocampo's "difficulty" in achieving literary expression might suggest that her writing is "different" or "inferior." Such assertions are reminiscent of a theory made popular by the work of Sandra Gilbert and Susan Gubar. Taking their cue from Harold Bloom's psychologized reading of literary history, and specifically his notion of the "anxiety of influence," Gilbert and Gubar elaborate their theory about women's "anxiety of authorship" in *The Madwoman in the Attic: The Woman Writer and the Nineteenth-Century Imagination:*

> Thus the loneliness of the female artist, her feelings of alienation from male predecessors coupled with her need for sisterly precursors and successors, her urgent sense of her need for a female audience together with her fear of the antagonism of male readers, her culturally conditioned timidity about self-dramatization, her dread of the patriarchal authority of art, her anxiety about the impropriety of female invention—all these phenomena of "inferiorization" mark the woman writer's struggle for artistic self-definition and differentiate her efforts at self-creation from those of her male counterpart. (50)

To suggest that women's writing is masked due to an "anxiety of authorship" implies that men's writing is free of such anxiety. It is to posit some centralized male writing made institutionally valid which women, by definition, cannot produce. Simultaneously, this suggestion conjures an essentialized female writing that women are somehow unable to unleash or unmask. We are left with a conundrum: women can neither write like men nor like women. Greenberg refers to the *Testimonios* as a parallel text to Ocampo's autobiography: Ocampo hides in the *Testimonios* and tells the truth in the autobiography ("Divided" 192). To argue that Ocampo uses male writing as a mask or screen, as Greenberg does, is to suggest that there is some "real" or "personal" expression hidden by the mask.[60]

Considering the *Testimonios* a mask for Ocampo's true expression provides fuel for the arguments of sexist critics who contend that "women's
writing is closer to their own personal experience than men's, that the female text *is* the author, or at any rate a dramatic extension of her unconscious" (Jacobus qtd. in Moi 61). It nicely supports the oft-made assertion
that women are only capable of writing about emotions. Such a view leads
to the familiar conflation of a woman (Ocampo) and her writing—a conflation we have seen made by Ortega y Gasset and Sábato—that serves to
diminish the circulation of ideas.

There is no room for change within the "anxiety of authorship" approach. Women are trapped forever in the male-dominated world of writing, able only to produce masked or doubled versions of their expressions.
As Toril Moi asserts, "Feminists must be able to account for the paradoxically productive aspects of patriarchal ideology (the moments in which the
ideology backfires on itself, as it were) as well as for its obvious oppressive
implications if they are to answer the tricky question of how it is that some
women manage to counter patriarchal strategies despite the odds stacked
against them" (64). Moi's comments suggest a more productive way to
approach Ocampo's writings. Rather than relegate the *Testimonios* to the
role of parallel autobiographical text, an approach centered on the "paradoxically productive" allows them to function as cultural criticism. We may
then state that this criticism, while marked by autobiographical characteristics, demonstrates a concern with the articulation of cultural values and
the social relevance of literary and artistic texts. A change in focus allows us
to avoid the essentializing trap involved in debating questions of anxiety,
masking, and originality. We are free to consider Ocampo as an agent making active use of her talents and to discuss how the ideology of patriarchy
backfired, emphasizing the fact that Ocampo took her private education
and put it to unexpected public use.

If we accept that Ocampo was always constructing her "I," it might be
useful to look at the *Testimonios* as a site where the focus is on using the "I"
(to translate, to edit, etc.) rather than constructing it. Ocampo expresses
concern with her historical/critical role. Considering herself a witness to a
cultural history that should be recorded, she is aware that writers construct
history differently, according to what we now call their own subjectivity. In
a prefatory note addressed to the reader in the sixth volume of *Testimonios*
she writes:

> [T]he articles and speeches from this new series [. . .] are not only in
> my drawers: they are in my diaries, in magazines and in the hands of
> some friends. It's not unlikely that it will occur to someone, when I'm

gone for good, to collect these dispersed pages. I would prefer to hasten and publish them myself, as insufficient as they seem to me. Moreover, it's not out of the question that these, like other testimonies, may serve at their time as points of reference.[61]

She believes that her interpretations form a part of Argentine history, and, though hers is an unpopular stance, she does not position herself as a disinterested observer. Ocampo considers her life, and that of her family and friends, to *be* that history. From this perspective, the autobiographical style of the *Testimonios* reflects a strategic choice on Ocampo's part rather than an anxiety about literary expression. She ties her criticism to her life, emphasizing its subjective nature precisely in order to make it personal and therefore as indisputable as her version of her life story. The result is a historical recording of one reader's engagement with literature and culture.

The first volume of the *Testimonios*, published in 1935, opens with a "Carta a Virginia Woolf." The letter is a mixture of Ocampo's memories of her visit to Woolf's house in London and a declaration of her writerly goals. In it she establishes the framework for what will eventually be ten volumes of letters, readings, and interviews published at approximately four-year intervals for the next forty years. The letter format of this piece is a stylistic conceit, a vehicle for Ocampo's particular style of literary criticism. Her choice of the letter and of other conventionally personal forms for writing about culture has likely contributed to the dismissal of her work as private and therefore undeserving of serious consideration as criticism. However, this drawing on the personal may be read as a demand that these "private" forms of writing be considered equally valid as conventionally "public" forms. Moreover, there is a freedom allowed by these personal forms which is often overlooked. Ocampo takes advantage of the openness of the letter format to combine her impressions of her visits with Woolf with glosses of Woolf's arguments and her own opinions of them. The result is a melding of subject and object that implies a critique of "objective" literary criticism.

Through her reading of Woolf, Ocampo addresses the position of the woman writer under patriarchy in this text, noting that she herself began to write while living in a "purely patriarchal society." She also summarizes Woolf's views on women's and men's writing as they are expressed in *A Room of One's Own*,[62] and agrees with her that women's written expression should be distinct from men's (12). These views lead her to criticize women writers like Anna de Noailles who consider themselves "exceptional" for their ability to write like men (15).

That Ocampo understood her work as a process of self-discovery is evident as she writes:

When seated next to your fireplace, Virginia, you drew me out of the mist and the solitude; when I stretched my hands toward the warmth and between us stretched a bridge of words . . . how rich it was, nevertheless! Not from your wealth, for that key which you found, and without which we never enter into possession of our own treasure (though we carry it throughout our lives hanging around our necks), can do me no good if I do not find it myself. Rich from my poverty, that is, from my hunger.[63]

Her search for the key to her own "treasure" has been portrayed in a negative light as evidence of an implied lack of quality in Ocampo's written expression. Though she exposes herself to such criticism by writing about her goals, Ocampo does not tie them exclusively to her own position as a woman writer. She explains that the articles in this volume "are a series of testimonies of my hunger. Of my so authentically American hunger!,"[64] identifying her hunger for expression as typically American. With further statements such as, "Like most uneducated south american women, I like writing,"[65] she places herself simultaneously within both identity groups. When Ocampo expresses her desire to write someday, "more or less poorly, but like a woman," she points to something beyond personal struggle.

A more general sense in which to understand her efforts is suggested by the closing lines of the "Carta": "And if, as you hope, Virginia, every effort, as dark as it may be, is convergent and hastens the birth of a form of expression that still has not found a climate favorable to its need to flower, may my force join that of as many women, unknown or renowned, as have worked in the world."[66] Here Ocampo joins her writing force with that of all women, placing herself within an international context. Such language does not suggest an image of the struggling, isolated woman writer.

It is clear, even from a cursory scan of the ten volumes of the *Testimonios,* that Ocampo focuses first and foremost on authors and artists whose work deals with Europe.[67] Even when Ocampo dedicates an entire segment of her book to "América," as she does in volume two of the *Testimonios,* twice as many of the essays in the collection are devoted to European authors and artists. The "Literatura" section of this volume, for example, contains the following pieces: "Virginia Woolf, Orlando y Cía.," "'Viaje olvidado'," "Emily Brontë (Terra incognita)," "Dette à la France," "Racine et Mademoiselle," and "Historia de mi amistad con los libros ingleses." The interest throughout Ocampo's writing remains focused clearly on Europe even as she advocates linkages between Latin America and the "Old World."

In volume three of the *Testimonios,* Ocampo addresses the granting of the Nobel Prize in literature to Gabriela Mistral. She lauds Mistral, mentioning her dedication to the Americas and her devotion to their indigenous peoples. Nonetheless, even as she praises Mistral—the first Latin American author to win the Nobel Prize—Ocampo cannot resist ending her essay on a note that highlights connection between Latin America and Europe: "Gabriela: the 'aubépines' [hawthorns] breathed by Proust that inundated him with a happiness without name, leaving him helpless, are neighbors of your almond trees. There isn't much distance, believe me, between Combray and your Valley of Elqui. My heart has measured the distance."[68]

Throughout the *Testimonios*, Ocampo consistently makes references that serve to place Europe and European culture at the center of her discursive world. She clearly privileges European writers as subjects of discussion. And from this perspective, two of the figures that loom large in her critical imagination are Virginia Woolf and Emily Brontë. It appears that it is these women—firmly ensconced in the tradition of British literary culture—with whom she identifies most closely.

The second volume of *Testimonios* contains two lengthy essays that address the work of these women authors. It is worth spending some time examining these essays for several reasons. Not only do they most clearly exemplify Ocampo's critical approach, they offer representative subject matter concerning European authors. Both were written originally as speeches and were subsequently published individually as short books prior to their inclusion in the *Testimonios*.[69] Finally, though they are considerably longer than most of her writings, these texts do not differ substantially in style from her other critical essays.

In the opening to the first essay, titled "Virginia Woolf, Orlando y Cía.," that she delivered to the "Amigos del Arte" in 1937, Ocampo informs her audience/readers: "I'm going to speak to you as a 'common reader' of the work of Virginia Woolf. I'm going to speak to you about the image I retain of her. Do not expect to hear pure literary criticism; you will be deceived."[70] These introductory remarks raise several questions. Is Ocampo apologizing? Are we, the audience, to expect part literary criticism and part something else or all "impure" literary criticism? What is "pure literary criticism"? Ocampo does not answer these questions, but her statements suggest that she herself considers her effort to be literary criticism of some variety.

The body of "Virginia Woolf, Orlando y Cía." is a blend of commentary on Woolf's novels and essays, defense of the common reader stance as Ocampo understands it, biographical material on Woolf, and Ocampo's recollections of discussions with and physical descriptions of Woolf. She describes English society at the time of Woolf's birth as dominated by "the most authoritarian woman we can imagine," the hypocritical Queen Victoria, who would suppress the rights of her female subjects (14). This brief biographical section brings to mind the parallel elements of Woolf's and Ocampo's biographies. Ocampo too considers herself a product/victim of a Victorian upbringing. In fact, both women were educated at home at the turn of the century, both became writers, both founded a press, and both wrote about gender and its inequalities.

From biography, Ocampo moves into a discussion of Woolf's works, beginning with *The Voyage Out*. She finds the novel to be of "quality," but written in a realist style that Woolf will abandon in her later novels. Citing Woolf, "Life is not a series of gig lamps symmetrically arranged; life is a luminous halo, a semi-transparent envelope surrounding us from the beginning of consciousness to the end," Ocampo aligns herself against realist writing and with a modernist aesthetic.[71]

It may be useful to contextualize Ocampo's preference for modernist writing, represented by her greater admiration of Woolf's later novels, within an Argentine framework. Much of the literary criticism published in Argentina in the 1920s appeared in the pages of such literary magazines as *Inicial, Martín Fierro, Proa, Los Pensadores, Claridad,* and *Síntesis.* Ocampo did not participate in the running of or contribute articles to these publications, but several of the consulting editors of *Sur,* namely Jorge Luis Borges, Eduardo Bullrich, Oliverio Girondo, and Eduardo Mallea, did.[72] These men were part of a group of writers and critics involved in what has become known as the "Boedo-Florida polemic." María Luisa Bastos points out that the situation was more complex than her description suggests, but she acknowledges that this "polemic" was basically one that pitted the "Florida" group of "ultraístas" or modernists of *Martín Fierro,* and later *Proa,* against the "Boedo" group of "realists" or leftists of *Los Pensadores* and later *Claridad* (64). It should be emphasized that the Boedo-Florida polemic involved men (with the exception of Norah Lange), a typical published exchange between the two groups including such barbs as, "To ask today, 'are you Boedo or Florida?'—is like saying, 'Are you a man or a fool?'"[73] Though Ocampo was not involved in this polemic, Bastos sees ties between the modernist *Proa* and *Sur.*

Amongst modernist writers internationally, Woolf, not surprisingly, is Ocampo's favorite. She considers *Mrs. Dalloway* (1925) to be Woolf's answer to her deliberations about what the novel should be and describes Clarissa Dalloway's story as "[t]he story of the past contained in the present to the breaking point, the story of its disturbing simultaneity. It is also the story of the invisible ties that connect human beings to one and other."[74] In her discussion of *Mrs. Dalloway,* Ocampo compares Woolf's use of memory with that of Proust. She also likens Proust, the writer, to Flush, Elizabeth Barrett Browning's dog. In Woolf's biography of Flush (titled *Flush*) the dog cannot understand why his mistress cries for what he considers to be no reason. His emotions are triggered only by sound and smell, and he can sense no provocation for his mistress's behavior (*Testimonios* 2 22). For Ocampo, Proust, like Flush, accesses the past through the senses of sound and smell while in Woolf's writing, vision, both inner and outer, is the primary sense. Though the writings of both exhibit a heightened sense of past, Ocampo finds their approaches distinct.

For Ocampo, Woolf's preoccupation with time comes to its full fruition in *Orlando,* the novel to which she devotes the bulk of her essay. Her discussion of the plot of *Orlando* foregrounds the position of the protagonist, Orlando, as reader and writer and the tension between the world of literature and the "real world": "And as life alone differs from life in literature just as green in nature differs from green in a poem, the existence of Orlando oscillates perpetually between these two poles, from the end of the sixteenth century to our day . . . "[75] Woolf's description of Orlando's engagement with literature is, for her, the best description of what the passion of reading can do to a person: "The discovery of a spirit through a book becomes an event of such magnitude in this being that it leaves him baffled with happiness for entire days, blind and deaf to all the rest."[76] Because the act of reading is of tremendous significance to Ocampo, Orlando the reader has a strong appeal for her.[77] Ocampo as reader is also drawn to what she calls the "most spiritual" of Woolf's passages, which depicts Orlando's deception upon meeting Alexander Pope. S/he discovers, in Ocampo's words, "that artists put their perfection in their works and not in their lives, outside themselves and not in themselves."[78] The parallels to Ocampo's own experiences with certain favorite authors are clear.[79] She suffered painful misunderstandings with several male authors who mistook her intellectual interest in them as sexual.

To emphasize the importance of the reader/writer and the power of reading in *Orlando,* Ocampo asks her audience to compare Woolf's writing to Colette's. She argues that it would be impossible for us to imagine Colette as a writer moving so easily from one place, sex, or time to another as Woolf does in *Orlando.* Such movement is possible for Woolf because the "anguish of the flesh" is not central to Woolf's work as it is to Colette's (54). Orlando, she argues, does not seem to live the love scenes in the novel: they are related in a detached way. Conversely, "Orlando doesn't *represent* his/

her passion for literature, his/her sense of the era and rebellion in the face of
the situation of inferiority imposed upon woman: Orlando lives them."[80]
Her comparison of Woolf and Colette (whom she praises in her own right)
suggests that Ocampo does not hold the stereotypical view that sensuality is
central to all women's writing. Her criticism of these and other authors
indicates her rejection of the common practice of branding women's writing
as homogeneous and inferior. Nor, as we have seen, does she shy away from
comparing Woolf's writing to that of male authors.

Women's gendered experience of society is highlighted in Ocampo's reading of *Orlando*. She notes the protagonist's sexual metamorphosis and the
insights it affords: "Female Orlando realized that women are neither naturally obedient, nor pure, nor perfumed, nor covered in adornments, and
that they only become that way by submitting themselves to the most both-
ersome discipline."[81] When Orlando feels the need to marry for support,
Ocampo points out that Woolf reassures the reader by blaming the
character's decision on the times: "it wasn't her, it was the century" (46).

For Ocampo, the gendered experience of society depicted in *Orlando* is
but one of the themes of Woolf's works. In her view, *The Common Reader*
indicates Woolf's love of books and authors; *A Room of One's Own* reveals
its author's concern with women's problems in general; *To the Lighthouse*
and *The Years* feature time as the principal protagonist. *Orlando* is most
interesting to Ocampo because it does some of each of these things (55). She
considers Woolf's writings as a whole and does not distinguish between
genres as she chooses her themes. Her positioning of *Orlando* as the synthe-
sis of these concerns serves in this essay as an introduction to her discussions
of Woolf's other writings.

Ocampo had read *The Common Reader* (1925) before her first volume
of *Testimonios* was published and was familiar with Woolf's critical essay
style. In his introduction to a 1983 edition of *The Common Reader*, Andrew
McNeillie characterizes that style: "For her part she was content to write, as
a reviewer, essays that share something of the immediacy, the flashing bril-
liance and unscholarliness of conversation in which (invariably unidentified) quotations are capped and a dinner-table intimacy is assumed" (xii).
McNeillie refers to this type of work as "impressionistic criticism." His
comments imply the existence of another, less impressionistic literary criticism distinct from Woolf's. The key evidence he provides for this claim is the
fact that Woolf's essays lack footnotes (which he provides in an appendix).

In his characterization of her style, McNeillie quotes John Gross's description of Woolf's criticism as "'a brilliant circular flight, which, as criti-

cism, leads nowhere'" and considers Gross's assessment to be "surprisingly close to Virginia Woolf's intention and design" (xiii). The essay form as employed by Woolf is thus viewed as an end in itself; not as criticism. Such a distinction indicates problems of definition for both the essay and literary criticism (or the essay as literary criticism). The placement of both Woolf and Ocampo within this field suggests a tendency to label critical writing by women as "essay" as opposed to "criticism." The appropriateness of a strict separation of the two is, however, questionable in a Latin American literary context where much critical writing has taken the essay form. McNeillie's introduction (1983) refers us for "general illumination" on the question of "impressionistic criticism" to T. S. Eliot's "The Perfect Critic" and "Imperfect Critics" in *The Sacred Wood* (1920). McNeillie's opinion of Woolf's critical approach seems too simplistic in its privileging of what he would call "scholarly" criticism.

Regardless of what label she attaches to her writing, Woolf finds her views on literature worth publishing. She concludes her essay, "The Common Reader," with a defense of what she argues is the common reader: "if he has, as Dr. Johnson maintained, some say in the final distribution of poetical honours, then, perhaps it may be worth while to write down a few of the ideas and opinions which insignificant in themselves, yet contribute to so mighty a result" (2). Ocampo does not discuss Woolf's "unscholarly" qualities as a critic, and she does refer to *The Common Reader* as a "book of criticism." Her analysis of Woolf's writing style suggests nothing but admiration for her approach. In particular, she praises the manner in which Woolf's critical writings invite dialog: "At each page we feel the desire to comment to the commentator through her commentary."[82] There is no suggestion that Ocampo finds Woolf's criticism lacking, and the words "impressionistic" and "unscholarly" do not appear in her essay.

Ocampo's defense of her own critical stance might be the same as her defense of Woolf's, for she invites the comparison.[83] She argues for the status of the common reader, trying to rescue the term from what she sees as its misinterpretation by the Italian futurist Filippo Marinetti, as signifying "the man in the street."[84] In connection with her remarks about Marinetti, Ocampo quotes from a letter José Ortega y Gasset published in *Espectador* in response to a letter she wrote to him expressing her concerns about her "reading style":

The way of reading practiced by you (what I would call in 1936 the way of the 'common reader') is not unjust and improper . . . It is, in

effect, the only way of reading that exists, the rest is erudition. Reading, in its most noble form, consists of a spiritual luxury, it is not study,
learning, acquisition of useful information for the social struggle. It is
a virtual growth and dilation that we offer to our interior germina-
tions; thanks to it we can realize that which throbbed only as a possibility in ourselves.[85]

According to Ortega y Gasset, Ocampo's reading is only for private/spiri-
tual purposes. No explicit reference is made to the act of writing about what
one reads. Meanwhile we should note that Ortega y Gasset expressed these
views on the private matter of reading in public(ation). In her own defense,
Ocampo suggests that both Marinetti and Ortega y Gasset are wrong about
the common reader. She denies that Woolf's (and her own) use of the term
is an affirmation of ignorance:

> To that title and under that title is how Virginia Woolf speaks to us
> of Montaigne, Defoe, Jane Austen, George Eliot, Addison, Conrad,
> Meredith, Hardy, Swift, the Brontë's, etc., and I can add that it is
> impossible to discover in her case any sign of ignorance.
> To speak in the name of the "common reader" was, then, a much
> less modest choice than what it might have appeared at first. If all the
> "common readers" were of the stature of Virginia Woolf, great writers
> would have no reason to complain about their public.[86]

Ocampo's conscious adoption of the common reader stance reveals a deliberate action as opposed to a mere reaction to her educational circumstance.
She chooses Woolf's writings as literary critical model. Essays on Woolf
appear throughout the volumes of the *Testimonios* and in her book *Virginia
Woolf en su diario* (1954). Ocampo actively introduced Woolf to the Span-
ish-speaking world by publishing translations of her works into Spanish
(through the Editorial Sur) beginning with the publication of Borges's translation of *Orlando* in 1936. It is important to note Ocampo's work on Woolf
not only for the writing itself, but also because there has been a tendency
among some critics of Ocampo to label her as a male hero-worshipper.[87]
    Ocampo is equally aggressive in her discussion of *A Room of One's
Own*, of which she says "[t]he problem of the woman as writer is dealt with
in those pages with extraordinary force and subtlety."[88] She emphasizes that
Woolf is not only interested in women as writers, but also in women's problems in general, regardless of class. Her remarks serve as an example of the
distinction Ocampo makes between feminism and politics. She does not
consider women's issues, as they relate to literature, as political. She notes:

"a leftist writer (and isn't it a disgrace that critics let their political passions show through when they talk about literature?) recently reproached Virginia Woolf for only describing, like Proust, the sufferings of the cream of the crop of the parasitic bourgeoisie."[89] The "crítico de izquierda" has erred, in Ocampo's thinking, because if her segment of society were to disappear, Woolf's work would remain as a valuable document. She points out, to reinforce her argument, that Woolf's Hogarth Press published working women's memoirs. Her defense of Woolf's writings as historical documents is reminiscent of Ocampo's views of the value of her own writings. At the same time, she denies what I consider to be the political nature of her own claims to public authority. By insisting on writing *like a woman* in public Ocampo, as Masiello puts it, "negotiates on behalf of a vast heterogeneity of citizen subjects who hope to enter the public arena without fear of losing their identity" (*Between* 158).

We again sense Ocampo's awkward separation of politics and literature when, in a digression, she contrasts Woolf's feminism to the "anti-feminism" of Queen Victoria and Anna de Noailles. She moves from these comments directly into discussion of male politicians in which she asserts, "it turns out to be difficult to admire Napoleon devotedly, to not find defects in him, and to believe at the same time in the emancipation of woman. I would like to add that this is also the case for Mussolini and for Hitler."[90] It seems that once the discussion is no longer explicitly literary, women's issues do count as political. These remarks are made in the context of a discussion of *A Room of One's Own*.

Ocampo concludes "Virginia Woolf, Orlando y Cía." with recollections of her encounters with Woolf. She depicts Woolf's face with the same terms she employs to describe her writing; "the enchantment of Virginia Woolf's face . . . enchantment of the happiest meeting of the material and the spiritual in the face of a woman."[91] For Ocampo, Woolf's beauty disproves the stereotypes of intelligent and talented women. It is not true that these women are "ugly or devoid of feminine charm; that every woman concerned with defending women's rights must be repulsive, unfortunate in marriage or a crazy old maid."[92] Again, when she moves from literature to the writer, Ocampo's remarks are more markedly feminist.

Ocampo's text reveals a fascination with both Woolf's writings and her person:

The prose that Virginia inhabits is thus . . . The chairs, the tables, the walls, the flower, the book, the shell, the Picasso that pass through her hands speak to us of her before and above all else. Why has she chosen this shell and not that other one? . . . What is she going to prefer? What is she going to underscore? Who will she come closest to? What does she tell us about the modern novel?[93]

This type of fascination is also what drives much of Ocampo's study of Emily Brontë, in which she also looks for connections between the life and person of the author and her writing.

"Emily Brontë (Terra Incógnita)," like "Virginia Woolf, Orlando y Cía.," was originally a speech and was delivered at the Biblioteca del Consejo de Mujeres" in June of 1938. Ocampo begins her remarks with a biographical sketch of the author, for Brontë, more so than Woolf, is a product of her environment: "If ever a human being were to be confused with the place of his or her birth and with its surrounding objects, it was without doubt Emily Brontë."[94] Ocampo directly equates the author with the characters in her novel, imagining that the atmosphere created in *Wuthering Heights* is the atmosphere in which Emily Brontë lived: "This book is a place, in the image of its title. But this place, marked on the maps of England, is more than England: it is the soul of Emily Brontë. The soul of Emily Brontë here in America and in whatever region of the world just as much as in England."[95] For Ocampo, *Wuthering Heights* is specifically Yorkshire, but in that specificity, it is also all lands: "In this way the most rooted in their land mix it with all lands. And perhaps I've never understood better what the great and harsh wind of the pampas with its cargo of wailing meant to me than when I heard the howl of the wind of *Wuthering Heights*."[96] Ocampo relates the novel to an Argentine setting, making an argument for its universality, based on its specificity. The logic behind her argument is that the novel is so rooted in its setting that it evokes a heightened awareness of his or her own surroundings in the reader.

The Brontë children spent much of their free time reading and writing, and Ocampo suggests that *Wuthering Heights* emerged from those childhood literary inventions. It is within the context of this discussion that she makes her oft-quoted remarks on the imagination of the writer:

> Each one of us carries within us the same scene, the same drama, from the moment of first consciousness and through the rest of our lives, and we perform our scene, our drama, whatever events or characters we may encounter, until we find our event, our character. We may never find them. But that doesn't stop us from performing our scene, our drama, and giving the events and the characters that are the least suitable for our scheme the form of the event and the character that are

our own. For each of us has come to the world for only one scene, only one drama, and we can't help but repeat them for all of our existence.[97]

The theatrical references here remind us of Ocampo's own formative years and her dramatic and writerly aspirations. The dramatic tone of the essay is highlighted by her invocation of Emily Brontë as if this were a seance: "The most direct way to enter into contact with her (besides her writings) is to make the inventory of all that surrounded her."[98] Her description, apparently based on Elizabeth Gaskell's biography of Charlotte Brontë, is one of a household controlled by a strict and domineering father in which the sole male offspring was favored.

Ocampo emphasizes the unequal treatment of the Brontë children. She mentions, for example, the fact that the Brontë sisters never told their brother they had published their writing so as not to humiliate him since he was meant to be their intellectual superior. They avoided telling their father as well: "'My father naturally held his son in higher esteem than his daughters,' says Charlotte"(105). Ocampo also repeats Gaskell's assertion that the boarding school in which the two eldest Brontë sisters died due to poor living conditions is described in *Jane Eyre*. She makes reference to her own childhood in her comments on this tragedy. Only materially spoiled children like herself, she claims, feel afflicted by lack of comprehension from adults. For poor children (like the Brontës), a tragedy such as death in the family is but one amongst more grave deceptions.

The poor treatment of women continues as a theme of the essay, and Ocampo repeats the notion that the Brontë sisters pretended that their brother Branwell was the family genius. She suggests that this was a fruitless conceit given that Branwell, even if he was intelligent, wasted his life on drugs and alcohol. Ocampo highlights the difficulties the Brontë sisters had with the literary establishment of their time, recounting the discouraging and sexist letter Charlotte received from a publisher and the sisters' subsequent decision to adopt masculine pseudonyms. Here Ocampo takes an opportunity to denounce the conditions that force women writers to protect themselves from "the repulsive mixture of condescension and praise still offered to women writers . . ."(127).

Returning to *Wuthering Heights,* Ocampo argues that it is a beautiful novel, but has no playfulness, humor, irony, or grace. Unlike Woolf and Austen, Emily (whom Ocampo conflates with the novel) does not smile nor does she make us smile, ever (143). In *Wuthering Heights,* "we feel the presence of those contradictory elements so characteristic of Emily Brontë:

her love of that which is limited and can therefore be named; her love for that which has no limits and, therefore, cannot be imprisoned in words, cannot be named."[99] The novel is thus an expression of Emily's personality: "When Heathcliff says to Nelly: 'My spirit is so eternally imprisoned, turned inward, that I am at times tempted to turn it outward, towards someone,' it is Emily who is telling us how and why *Wuthering Heights* has been written."[100]

As a part of her biographical approach to literature, on full display in this essay, Ocampo divides writers into two groups: "Great artists produce, in my understanding, two types of work according to their nature and with the circumstances of their life: some are compensatory, the others complementary."[101] She characterizes two contemporary women authors, Anna de Noailles and Colette, to illustrate her point. All writing is both compensatory and complementary, but one tendency usually prevails. Noailles's work is compensatory because she wrote about things that she did not live. For example, she wrote poetry about nature but, according to Ocampo, could not stand to be out-of-doors: "Anna de Noailles the poet who wrote and the woman whom one met seemed like two different beings."[102] Collette, on the other hand, is the typical complementary writer: "One feels that in life she enjoys with pleasure what she continues to enjoy in her books. We pass from the woman to the work, from the work to the woman, without staggering."[103] The same is true of Woolf, she argues. Emily Brontë, like Noailles, is predominantly a compensator though her work contains some complementary elements. The complementary aspect of her writing is that she never describes the moors; they are expressed as a prolongation of her self (157). But, "she only dared to live according to her temperament through them. Her passion, her violence, her tumult bursts in them, breaks in them all the barriers with a force even more terrible in that it finds no other outlet."[104] By living her passions through her characters, Brontë is compensating.

This essay, in addition to its life as a speech, also served as the preface to the first Argentine edition of *Wuthering Heights*. Its final section is specifically designed to reach the reading public that will include not only those who read the Argentine edition of *Wuthering Heights*, but also those who read the *Testimonios* in which it is reprinted. Here Ocampo calls to the dead Emily Brontë to tell her that Heathcliff is home: "Because Heathcliff was an unsociable child and had brown skin, the evil tongues said of him: 'An american or spanish castaway'—an abandoned American or Spaniard. Here, then, Heathcliff is at home. Here, is America and still Spain."[105] Ocampo tells Brontë that her book is now in the distant mysterious land she may have seen on her father's map (165). Through the device of calling to Brontë from her present, Ocampo positions Latin America, naming that mysterious, marginal place, confirming that it exists and that real people live and write in it. Ocampo identifies with Heathcliff, the dark other of *Wuthering Heights,* claiming a Latin American home for him.

In this final section, Ocampo asks that her audience forgive her involuntary errors: "I would like, here, to ask your pardon since my love for her is exact. Exact like all that is love and not curiosity."[106] Her plea serves as a reminder that Ocampo's is not in any way meant to be a distant or "objective" look at Brontë's work.

An approach to literature based entirely on the author's personality can be painfully narrow, but Ocampo's attention to the connections between an author's life and his or her writing is neither exclusive nor does she leave these observations undeveloped. A biographical approach is the framework upon which she constructs much broader arguments. Her work is not strictly based on grouping by country, for example. In fact, Ocampo moves effortlessly from one literature or language to another, often translating for her readers as she goes. It is possible that her avoidance of groupings, national or otherwise, is a product of Ocampo's attempt to maintain a separation between literature and politics. As we have seen in the case of her feminist views, this approach is not always successful.

In the conclusion of "The Divided Self," Janet Greenberg attributes the conflicts in Ocampo's writings to her lack of confidence in her opinions. In my view, Ocampo successfully inhabited the structures of power available to her. Her attempt to gain interpretive power within a patriarchal society obviously had its price. Her *Testimonios* should be read, as Emir Rodríguez Monegal suggests, as "the chronicle of a woman who, in a country of condescending machos, dared to think and to feel and to love as she saw fit."[107]

Ocampo took Paul Groussac's advice and used it to more advantage than he would ever have imagined. When he suggested, "Why . . . don't you choose another less Dantesque, not to say pedantic, type of subject if you really feel you must write? For example, personal experiences lived by you, etc." (qtd. in Ocampo, *Testimonios* 5 22), Ocampo did. She wrote about personal experience, but it was her personal experience of literature as literary criticism, precisely the sanctified type of writing from which Groussac tried to exclude her.

4

Nation and Motherhood
in Gabriela Mistral

According to Victoria Ocampo, John Ruskin "said that the most marvelous spectacle of all—a spectacle superior to that of a perfect work of art—consists of the sight of a beautiful human creature 'who also has a brain'."[1] Though this particular beautiful human creature is not marked as feminine, such a description echoes frequent turn-of-the-century comparisons between women's bodies and works of art that position woman primarily as physical object. A reversal of the customary gender position involving viewer and object opens Ocampo's essay, "Al margen de Ruskin: algunas reflexiones sobre la lectura," in which she discusses one of the three speeches in Ruskin's 1865 collection *Sesame and Lilies*. Here, Ocampo makes the English critic the subject of her gaze as she meditates on his portrait: "when one observes that face of a rare material and spiritual beauty, it is impossible to avoid thinking that no one better than Ruskin himself should have deserved that phrase he dedicated to others: 'A splendid thing to look at, an admirable thing to speak to'."[2] The reversal discloses her purpose: though Ocampo praises Ruskin in general terms by suggesting that dialogue with him is admirable,[3] her essay is a specific response to what she reads as his attack on the reader in "Sesame: Of Kings' Treasures."

For Ocampo, as we know, the reader is integral to the literary process. Consequently, she takes particular issue with Ruskin's positioning of the reader in relation to the author: "If the person who wrote the book is not wiser than you, you need not read it; if he be, he will think differently from you in many respects" (Ruskin 20). Ever mindful of the reader's position in her defense of the "common reader," Ocampo bristles at Ruskin's treatment: "how can he ignore that there are occasions in which the reader shouts with reason: 'How good this is! It is exactly what I think!' without having for it the knowledge of the author whose book he reads?"[4] Ocampo does not go so far as to suggest that the reader and the author are equal. However, Ruskin's insistence that the reader must suffer to truly understand the text and must humble himself before the authors of "the court of the past" runs counter to her emphasis on the pleasure of the act of reading. With its informal tone, Ocampo's critical approach is one that seems to encourage the easy approximation of reader and work rather than the distance implied by Ruskin's positionings.[5]

In her turn, Gabriela Mistral also casts her gaze upon Ruskin, but to entirely different effect in *Lecturas para mujeres*. Edited by Mistral and published by the Mexican Ministry of Education in 1923, this reader contains four pieces by Ruskin, including the segment of "Of Kings' Treasures" discussed by Ocampo in her essay. Their treatments of Ruskin are emblematic of Mistral and Ocampo's differing approaches to the relationship between reader and writer. Though the *Lecturas* are intended for didactic purposes, Mistral provides no analysis of the works she includes in the text. Instead, her preface to the reader and her selection of writings constitute the basis for my critical analysis. Her use of Ruskin's work in particular points to questions and comparisons that might provide a framework for the study of the *Lecturas:* What place did Mistral intend for the reader of this collection? What is revealed by her opening a textbook directed toward women in post-revolutionary Mexico with a fragment of Ruskin's "Lilies: of Queens' Gardens," a speech written fifty years earlier and considered old-fashioned even by Victorian standards (Kirchhoff 101)?[6] From what cultural context and set of assumptions about women's education did the text emerge? Finally, what insight does it provide into Mistral's views on women and literature? As a means of approaching these questions and Mistral's role as literary and cultural critic, it may be useful to place her image as it comes to us through traditional literary criticism.

Born Lucila Godoy Alcayaga in Vicuña, Chile, in 1889, Mistral is one of the best known Latin American women writers of the twentieth century, and her fame is framed by two primary considerations. On the one hand, her winning the Nobel Prize for literature in 1945 has led most studies of her work to center almost exclusively on her poetry. The prevailing public image of Mistral is filled with ironies: she is enshrouded in myths of maternity and heterosexuality. Mistral has been fixed in a maternal role, a process succintly described by Alberto Sandoval Sánchez: "Woman-mother-maternity have become synonyms of the the mistraline poetic message as a result of the patriarchal and paternalistic valoration of her person and her poetic production."[7] This valuation of the maternal both stems from and generates the nearly exclusive attention given to her lullabies and poems for children. The result has been a narrowly accepted view of her poetry, one that excludes alternative readings of her canonized poems and ignores those that do not address maternal themes. Consequently, much of her other poetry has been left unexplored.

Recent rereadings have sought to work against this maternal stereotype. Among them is Licia Fiol-Matta's "The 'Schoolteacher of America': Gender, Sexuality and Nation in Gabriela Mistral" (1995). As Fiol-Matta notes, even feminist readings have evaded the topic of sexuality in Mistral's works. Her rereading proposes that Mistral's manipulation of representations of women allows her both to hide and to articulate lesbian identity and desire (202). I will elaborate on the manipulations of Mistral's image below. Another re-evaluation is Sylvia Molloy's translation and analysis of Mistral's "Electra en la niebla," a poem of matricide. In a reworking of the classical story, Mistral makes Electra responsible for Clytemnestra's death ("Introduction" 113, 133–136), thus transforming Electra and not her brother Orestes into the responsible agent of revenge.[8] The present discussion is driven by a similar desire to rethink Mistral's work and her position as a woman writer. In particular, I mean to examine her very public and conflicted role as teacher and—most pertinent to this study—cultural critic.

In large part, Mistral's role is scripted by her historical and institutional situation. *Lecturas para mujeres* was published in 1923 by the Mexican Ministry of Education. Mistral had gone to Mexico in 1922, invited by the government of Alvaro Obregón to work for the Ministry of Education in a program of educational reform. When Obregón assumed the presidency in December of 1920, nearly two-thirds of Mexico's population of 14 million was illiterate. In 1921, his Minister of Education, José Vasconcelos, began a large-scale campaign designed to bring education to rural children and illiterate adults throughout Mexico.

Vasconcelos concentrated his efforts on primary education in rural areas. Over one thousand rural schools were built in Mexico between 1920 and 1924, as were two thousand libraries (Meyer and Sherman 573–574). Teachers were sent to act as educational missionaries who would, according to Vasconcelos, "imitate the action of the colonial Catholic missionaries amongst the Indians who still are not familiar with the castillian language."[9] Vasconcelos oversaw the reprinting of Roman and Greek classics as reading material for the newly literate, many of whom were indeed Amerindians. These texts were widely distributed by the newly established mobile libraries and public schools. "And where should he who wants to make others read begin?" he asks. "Is there an educated person in the world who denies that the beginning of all cultured reading is in the classic authors of Humanity?"[10] Though its main concern was nationalist—including the affirmation of Mexico's indigenous cultures—at the heart of Vasconcelos' literacy program lay the classic texts associated with European culture.

The same can be said for his approach to education in general. Writing in his autobiography about educational reform, Vasconcelos disdains the importation of North American schoolteachers, a practice undertaken by the Argentine educator Domingo Faustino Sarmiento (F. Miller *Latin* 46). Instead, he values European culture over what he sees as imperialist North American culture. This is evident in the relative positions of Mexico, North America, and Europe in his critique of Sarmiento's educational reforms:

> When Sarmiento consummated his educational work in Argentina, first he learned Horace Mann by heart; next, in case he was forgetting something, he carted in two or three hundred North American teachers and set them up in the pampa [. . .] But Mexico's case was different. Mexico had a University before Boston, and libraries, museums, newspapers and theater, before New York and Philadelphia. In Mexico it is enough to scratch the surface a little to unearth the sprouts of the old culture, buried by the barbarity of the governments.[11]

Though he rejects the importation of North American teachers and teaching models, Vasconcelos advocates employing Mexican teachers with European training. As in his preference for reading materials, he looks to Europe as the source of knowledge and culture. And his system of evaluation is based on age: Europe has an older culture than Mexico, whereas North America's is even younger. Interestingly enough, though ancient, Amerindian culture is excluded from his relative scale of cultural value.

Although she claimed some Amerindian heritage herself, Mistral shared Vasconcelos's cultural views. She too looked to Europe as a model. She once wrote to a friend, "All that I know, little, but very fertile in my life, she, Europe, has given to me."[12] Within the institutional practices Vasconcelos established to bring literacy to Mexico, Mistral found a powerful affirmation of her own cultural values.

In her introduction to the *Lecturas para mujeres* titled, "Gabriela Mistral (1922–1924)," Palma Guillén de Nicolau recalls the atmosphere in Mexico City during Vasconcelos's tenure as Minister of Education:

> In the Capital, the Secretary of Education was editing the Greek classics, Plotinus, the Gospels and the Divine Comedy and in the Amphi-

theater of the Preparatory, decorated by Diego Rivera and chockfull, we listened to Beethoven's Symphonies. Now it was necessary to redo and to sow, to institute the order of justice and of culture and, just as the campesinos go to the field with their sacks of seeds, so did Vasconcelos send us everywhere—each to do what he knew, or to practice what he was dreaming, or to learn, for, in the end, everything was necessary for the people hungry for bread and for culture.[13]

Guillén de Nicolau describes a city alive with cultural renewal and growth. This passage also overtly suggests a parallel between lack of food and lack of culture. The "people" appears devoid of its own culture, yearning to be nourished with European literature and music as much as it yearns for food. Vasconcelos's campaign workers, European classics in hand, will sow the field of cultural production, will reap the benefits of European civilization planted in the fertile terrain of the New World.

The literacy campaign in which Guillén de Nicolau and Mistral participated was part of a broad educational program that included both classic Greco-Roman literature and contemporary Mexican visual arts. Diego Rivera, José Orozco, David Alfaro Siqueiros, and others were encouraged by Obregón's government to create art that would instruct on a popular level. The relationship of Latin American art to that of Europe was central to these visual artists' work. As such, they engaged actively with the problem of "authenticity" in the creation of their art. Rivera, in particular, attempted to replace a Eurocentric aesthetic with an indigenous one. Oriana Baddeley and Valerie Fraser suggest that the muralists were more politically engaged and their projects more radical than Vasconcelos had expected:

In the wake of the Mexican Revolution Vasconcelos aimed to utilize the skills of his country's artists as part of a more general programme of popular education. Once given access to the walls of public buildings, however, Rivera, Orozco and Siqueiros proceeded to develop their own particular blend of aesthetics and radical politics which was frequently at odds with those of their government patrons. (81)[14]

The muralists brought to the foreground the political nature of art and challenged Mexico's cultural dependence on North America and Europe. Though Vasconcelos may have agreed with them in their resistance to North American imperialism, their critiques of the unbalanced relationship between Europe and Mexico must have troubled him and the government for which he worked.[15]

Vasconcelos and many of those who had a voice in the Mexican government during the 1920s came largely from the Mexican middle class. Though they supported some common goals of the Revolution, most did not advocate the radical change envisioned by the muralists. Indeed, Obregón's presidency reflected this conservative approach. Through backing the conservative CROM (Confederación Regional Obrera Mexicana), he shut out rival union groups and their aggressive demands for the labor reform called for under Article 123 of the 1917 Constitution. He also ignored demands for agrarian reform, carrying out only a fraction of the redistribution of land called for in Article 27.[16] And, conveniently, Pancho Villa, the Revolution's last popular peasant rebel, was executed under "mysterious" circumstances in 1923. While political opposition was violently suppressed, Obregón maintained the support of military leaders and other politicians by tolerating corruption that produced an extremely wealthy "revolutionary" elite (O'Malley 13).[17] In this political context, the educational reforms implemented by Vasconcelos represent a relatively progressive element of Obregón's presidency. Furthermore, Vasconcelos was advocating education of both men and women of all classes.

Prior to the institution of Vasconcelos's program, the majority of women who received education in Mexico were of the upper classes and were taught in private, mostly Catholic, schools that were practically non-existent outside of urban centers. From 1922 to 1924, Gabriela Mistral worked for the Ministry of Education under Vasconcelos helping to organize programs in rural areas, overseeing the introduction of mobile libraries, and establishing *escuelas hogar* for women. These schools, as their name suggests, were aimed specifically at homemakers as opposed to those geared toward normal-school teachers. Their education as homemakers followed a period in which women contributed in various ways to revolutionary change.

Many Mexican women were forced into non-traditional roles by the Revolution in which they participated as spies, smugglers, combatants, providers of food, nurses, etc. Others entered the labor pool to offset the labor shortage brought on by conscription (Meyer and Sherman 557). Women were also active in feminist groups that fought for social and legal reform. In 1916, two feminist conferences that centered on suffrage as a means of social reform were held in Mérida (F. Miller *Latin* 76). The rhetoric of the Revolution promised political participation for all Mexican citizens. As Francesca Miller notes, however, women were officially excluded from the benefits of the Revolution: "The Mexican Constitutional Convention met at Querétaro in December 1916 and in ten months produced the Mexican Constitution of 1917, hailed as the most advanced social and political document of its day. Political rights, including the right to vote, were granted to all Mexican citizens; *women were excluded from the category of citizen*" (77, my emphasis). The official fruits of the Revolution were thus denied to at least half of the Mexican population, denied—more importantly—to a segment of the population directly responsible for its success.

Though it could not have succeeded without them, the official discourse of the Revolution both denied women the rights of citizenship and restricted them to the traditional domestic sphere. Their primary role was to produce future national citizens. In fact, in April of 1930, the *Excelsior* in Mexico City ran a "Most Prolific Mother" contest instead of the usual commemoration of the death of Emiliano Zapata.[18] As Ilene O'Malley shows in her study of hero cults and the institutionalization of the Revolution, the relationship between revolutionary male comrades was often idealized. An excerpt from the Mexican periodical *El Popular* serves as an example: "And to the comrade, oh! The comrade! . . . to him is owed a sacred place in the heart, . . . to love him as a brother, . . . to unite your emotions, your pleasures, and your sufferings and thus you will be a single soul that feels, . . . a single intelligence that thinks, a strong potent whole, capable of carrying out actions that transcend glory . . ."[19] The author describes and glorifies a fraternal bond between equals, emphasizing empathy and shared experience.

On the other hand, the relationship between the revolutionary soldier and his female counterpart, the *soldadera*, was marked by its distinct inequality in a poem recommended by the Partido Nacional Revolucionario for inspirational readings at civic ceremonies. The poem is "La soldadera":

> You have deadened your feet
> on the stones of the road;
> Your belly is rent
> by a barbarous tenderness,
> multiplier of births;
> on the rags over your teats
> have been hung
> those crucified in this agrarianist hour;
> with your blood full of bacteria
> you have filled with Nazarene sons,
> as if with seeds,
> the furrows of the Revolution;

and your sanctified brown flesh
opened at the command of Emiliano Zapata.
Because you gave birth to our children in the streets
or in prison;
because the victors possessed you
and we lost you in the pillage of all the disasters
when you were carrying our children in your flesh;
because they filled you with excretions
and hanged you from the trees,
because many like you stayed behind rotting
in the middle of the road . . .
and because you
like us,
have gambled your life . . .

> Sister *soldadera,*
> Blessed art thou![20]

"La soldadera" reveals in graphic detail how some women were active participants in and victims of war. The activity most highly praised, however, is the woman's sacrifice of her body. Emphasis is placed on motherhood which, in this case, is depicted as a response to Zapata's command. Throughout, the *soldadera* is a passive vessel/object possessed or lost by men. Here, Mary Louise Pratt's description of the role afforded women within the modern nation seems particularly apt: "They are practically forbidden to be limited and finite, being obsessively defined by their reproductive capacity. Their bodies are sites for many forms of intervention, penetration, and appropriation at the hands of the horizontal brotherhood" (51). In referring to the nation as a "horizontal brotherhood," Pratt elaborates on Benedict Anderson's description of the modern nation he articulates in *Imagined Communities: Reflections on the Origin and Spread of Nationalism.* Anderson argues that the nation is imagined as limited, as sovereign, and as a community: "[I]t is imagined as a *community,* because, regardless of the actual inequality and exploitation that may prevail in each, the nation is always conceived as a deep, horizontal comradeship" (16). There is no public role for women within this articulation of the nation. Thus the *soldadera* is treated differently from the comrade. She can never be publicly acknowledged as an agent of the Revolution despite her active participation in it.

No mention of the *soldadera* or the Revolution is made in Mistral's *Lecturas* despite the fact that it was published under the auspices of the

Mexican government. In fact, the public sphere in general and the political in particular are conspicuously absent from the writings Mistral collects in this volume. They are not, however, absent from the circumstances of its production. In her 1966 introduction to the Porrúa edition of the *Lecturas* (as of 1988, the book was in its seventh edition) Palma Guillén de Nicolau tells us that Mistral rushed to finish the text and its introduction so that she could leave Mexico as quickly as possible. According to Guillén de Nicolau, she had become aware of a feeling of public resentment against her for being summoned to Mexico from abroad. Guillén de Nicolau attributes this attitude to nationalism and reminds the reader, "do not forget that we are very nationalistic" (ix). Resentment apparently surfaced when it was learned that Vasconcelos planned to name an *escuela hogar* after Mistral and had commissioned Ignacio Asúnsolo to make a statue of her for the school's patio (ix–x). The unpleasant circumstances under which she prematurely left her post come through in Mistral's own "Introducción a estas *Lecturas para mujeres,*" which she opens with the phrase *"Palabras de la extranjera,"* marking her own position as outsider.

As "the foreigner" explains in her introduction, she was asked by Vasconcelos to edit a book of "Scholastic Readings." Though Vasconcelos clearly had a broader purpose in mind, Mistral claims a tiny audience for the *Lecturas*: "I comprehended that making a text is a task for national teachers and not a foreigner, and I have compiled this work only for the Mexican school that bears my name."[21] By making such a restricted claim, Mistral at once draws attention to and attempts to distance herself from the nationalistic atmosphere in which the text was produced. The strategy of calling attention to potentially problematic aspects of her own work is, as we shall see, a deflective technique Mistral employs throughout her more public prose pieces.

Assuming that her female students will not study the humanities elsewhere, Mistral hopes to provide them with a small portion of the artistic culture she feels a woman should possess (xiii). In her discussion of the task of editing/*recopilando* examples of that culture, she continues to both invoke and deflect the national:

> My little work does not pretend to compete with the national texts, of course: it has the logical defects of the work done by a traveller. . . . A book of this type is, in my judgement, a work of three years and requires much tranquility of spirit and a profound understanding of the environment. This is the rehearsal of a work that I will one day carry out in my country, destined for all the women of America. I feel

they are my spiritual family; I write for them, perhaps without preparation, but with much love.[22]

She articulates here a view of America which stretches beyond the borders of Mexico and well beyond the walls of her school. In so doing, Mistral moves away from the problem of the "national" (which is associated with the masculine, the "horizontal brotherhood") by positing a familial bond with a broader female, "American" readership. Like Ocampo, she also mentions her own lack of education in a preemptive gesture that seems designed to raise the issue of her credentials before it is raised by potential critics.[23] Elizabeth Horan reads this as a survival strategy for Mistral who, she observes, "continuously defers to the social and cultural elite that permits her to speak" (*Gabriela* 11).

The *Lecturas* represent the only sustained collection of writings including prose and poetry whose shape was fully determined by Mistral. Her other prose writings were published individually through newspapers and only anthologized after her death.[24] Dispersed as this other body of work is, it is difficult to characterize these pieces as a unified text. Many of them were sold as occasional articles to newspapers and magazines. While favoring Latin America, Mistral's articles privilege a European canon. They reflect many of the same concerns that are voiced in the *Lecturas,* but do not represent a sustained discussion of social issues. As several critics note, these occasional writings were produced over a long period of time, in various locations, and written during lengthy periods of travel. René Letona has noted that many of them had the "ephemeral condition of journalism."[25]

Only the *Lecturas para mujeres* stand as a sustained statement from Mistral concerning the articulation of cultural values and the social relevance of literary texts. The *Lecturas* are an intervention in the social and educational development of a revolutionary Latin American country. As such, they are directly engaged with the development of a national culture. They represent a text for and about women produced by a woman and are implicated, therefore, in the discussions about women as cultural subjects and producers of knowledge within the arena of nation building and politics.

An attentive reading of Mistral's introduction provides a road map to the *Lecturas.* What emerges is a sense of her paradoxical engagement with the national, paradoxical because her position implicitly critiques the absence of women in discourses of nationalism while calling up the conservative position that women maintain traditionally inscribed gender roles. As a mark of women's absence in the national discourse, she expresses concern about the lack of readings directed toward women in school primers and, specifically, the absence of material that pertains to the subject of mother-hood, the sole purpose of women's being: "And be she a professional, a worker, a *campesina* or a just a lady, her only reason for being on this earth is maternity, both material and spiritual, or the latter in the case of we women who do not have children."[26] In order to address this lack, Mistral includes a section in the *Lecturas* titled "Hogar" containing pieces that exalt motherhood and the home and in her words, "that make felt, ennobled, the ambience of the house" (xiii). By use of what quickly becomes a familiar strategy, Mistral has both drawn attention to and deflected the fact that she herself is not a mother.

Her insistence on motherhood as the central focus of women's lives must be read as an attempt to conserve patriarchal social order.[27] At the same time, however, Mistral's prescriptions reveal a move to connect women of disparate social groups through the domestic sphere. By linking women's identity to domesticity, her strategy sidesteps the male-identified public sphere. The home, she suggests, demarcates a female space—one distinctly separate from men's sphere—over which women have complete control. The home thus becomes a place of resistance to patriarchal public order. Not surprisingly, she expresses an anxiety about the modern breakdown of that domestic sphere: "Perhaps in no small part the *Reading Books* without a feminine disposition have contributed to that type of dimming of the family spirit that one sees in the younger generations."[28] Despite her calls to resist the dissolution of the home, Mistral's traditional view is not as un-complicated as it might appear. She does not wish, for example, to deny women their newly achieved independence: "The participation, each day more intense, of women in the liberal and industrial professions brings an advantage: their economic independence, an indisputable good; but it also brings a certain disintegration of the home, and, above all, a slow loss of the sense of maternity."[29] Recognizing women's economic independence from men as positive, Mistral is nonetheless uneasy about the contemporary de-cline of the "sense of maternity" which, as we shall see, she invests with a certain type of privilege and power. The disintegration of bonds between men and women arising from an increase in women's activities outside the home does not particularly concern her. Rather, the bonds between mother and child lie at the core of Mistral's critique.

In her discussion of the disintegration of the home, Mistral sets up a contrast between the so-called "mujer nueva" (new woman) and the woman she vaguely refers to as the "mujer antigua" (ancient woman). Though she declines to name her in the Introduction, the *mujer antigua* appears later in the *Lecturas* as the ancient Roman or Hebrew woman in the selection "A la mujer mexicana," a printed version of a speech Mistral gave at the Congreso Mexicano del Niño in 1923.[30] Here, she encourages women to look to the mothers of antiquity for role models:

> Mexican mother: in searching for your great models, do not look to the crazy women of this century who dance and move about in plazas and salons and barely know the child they carried inside them, the stingy women who betray life by avoiding duty without having avoided pleasure. You will look to the ancient and eternal models: to the Hebrew mothers and the Roman mothers.[31]

These exhortations harken back to an age in which Mistral imagines gender roles were stable and bonds between women and children were privileged. In this fictive world, men do not inhabit the domestic scene and women maintain uninterrupted bonds with their children: "[Y]ou do not have to renounce the thousand nights of anguish next to your feverish child, nor do you have to permit the mouth of your child to drink the milk of a mercenary breast. You will nurse, you will rock, you will go carrying the thyrsus of jasmines that life let fall upon your breast."[32] The woman to whom these lines are addressed is told by Mistral to remain with her children. The *mujer antigua,* she argues, had a deeper sense of motherhood, a sense that is threatened by the encroachment of the modern world as personified by the traitorous *mujer nueva,* who would leave the domestic space and break the bonds between mother and child. As they re-valorize activities associated with motherhood, Mistral considers the *Lecturas,* specifically collected for homemakers and future homemakers, as an act of resistance to the modern disintegration of the family. She envisions a world of cohesive families in which the home is sacred. The power of men, however, does not take hold in this space. The home becomes the site of women's power, the place where the fulfillment of women's role ignores—finally—the real power relationships between men and women in families. This seeming lack of grounding in the socio-historical realities of early-twentieth-century Latin America is curious. Indeed, to provide an adequate reading of the *Lecturas,* it is imperative to understand the relationship between women, education, and nationalism at the time Mistral's text was published.

In one sense, the motherhood role Mistral advocates for women constitutes a perpetuation of views on women's education established in Latin America in the nineteenth century. For some educators, arguments for formally educating women were based upon their role as the reproducers and educators of future national citizens. To their minds, women could be allowed training as teachers because teaching was an extension of women's traditional role as mother. Young women were to be educated so that they would mother good citizens. The opinions of Justo Sierra, a late-nineteenth-century predecessor of José Vasconcelos in Mexico, exemplify this view:

> The educated woman will be truly one for the home; she will be the companion and the collaborator of man in the formation of the family. That is what we want and that is what you are being so firmly morally prepared for here . . . You are called to form souls, to sustain the soul of your husband; for this reason, we educate you. *Niña querida,* do not turn feminist in our midst . . . No, you and ourselves are mutually complementary; we form a single personality called to continue the perpetual creation of the nation.[33]

Sierra's paternalistic tone is characteristic of the nationalistic motives underlying the initial push to educate women in Latin America. That Mistral's view should coincide with those of her anti-feminist nineteenth-century male predecessors indicates the conservatism of her views. Yet, the above citation does point to one difference between them. Whereas Sierra explicitly mentions women's duty to sustain their husbands, husbands are rare in the pieces Mistral selects for the *Lecturas* and are entirely absent from her own writing in the collection. Mistral envisions, in the *Lecturas,* a space in which women form to some degree their own "horizontal sisterhood," free from the control of male partners though fully under the command of the patriarchal order to be fruitful and multiply.

Still, Mistral's views on women's education are anachronistic, setting her apart from many of her schoolteaching female predecessors and contemporaries who advocated educational (as well as legal) equality of the sexes. Francesca Miller describes their activities around the turn of the century:

> Whereas many of the early proponents of women's rights in Latin America were upper-class women, speaking out as individuals, it was female schoolteachers who formed the nucleus of the first women's groups to articulate what may be defined as a feminist critique of society, that is, to protest against the pervasive inequality of the sexes in legal status, access to education, and political and economic power. . . . The emergence of a collective female critique of discriminatory practices based on gender is well illustrated in the discussions of the series of scientific conferences held in the Southern Cone between 1898 and 1909. . . . They [women] presented papers on health care, hygiene, child care, nutrition, mother welfare, and botanical and biological research, as well as the divisive issue of equal education. The

debate over female education began in a discussion of what kinds of education were suitable for women. The women delegates were indignant that the debate should be cast in these terms, insisting on the need for equal facilities for all. The debate gradually broadened into a wide-ranging attack on the pervasive inequality of the sexes within society (*Latin* 71–72).

Miller's research suggests that a discourse of equality in education was already established in international feminist circles and particularly amongst female schoolteachers ten years before Mistral went to work in Mexico. Though it may be argued that to advocate education for women was at that time more progressive than to maintain the status quo, Mistral's views appear far more conservative than radical within the context of the ongoing educational debate described by Miller. Mistral is not, for example, arguing for equal educational facilities for men and women.[34] As Miller puts it, "her emphasis was to better prepare women to fulfill their traditional roles as mothers and homemakers, not to seek new roles" (*Latin* 59). Indeed, Mistral laments the fact that boys and girls use the same books in school (*Lecturas* xiii).

In her introduction to the *Lecturas*, Mistral makes reference to the need for a broader education for women that would address issues pertinent to a proper household including maternity and what she calls "the great human topics." These topics—social justice, work, and nature—form three key subjects treated in the *Lecturas*. Mistral allows that the education of the otherwise superior *mujer antigua* was lacking in these areas due to her restricted (domestic) ideals. Despite the gesture in the direction of breadth, the actual selections appearing in the anthology are only vaguely related to their purported topics. For example, the "Trabajo" section includes the following "Himno Matinal de la 'Escuela Gabriela Mistral' de México," written by the poet herself:

Oh, Creator; beneath your light we sing
because once again you give us hope.
Like the furrows of the earth we raise
the exhalation of our praise.

Thank you for the glorious day
in which deeds will be raised;
for the dawn full of happiness
that descends on the valley and the hearts.

Hands are raised, those that you made,
fresh and lively over the chores.

Arms are raised, that you bathed with light,
in an ardent tremor of beehives.
    We are still nurseries of daughters;
make our souls righteous and powerful
so that we are worthy on the great day
on which we will be the nursery of wives.
    Watch us create in your profound image
with will distinguished in beauty;
weaving, weaving divine with confidence,
the white flax with the pure wool.
    Watch us cut the wheat from the stalk;
put the fruits on the bright table;
weave the sedge that is our friend:
Create, create gazing upon your beauty!
    Oh, Creator of supreme hands,
the fruit rises in the anxious song,
that now we are the nursery of sisters,
but we will be the nursery of wives.[35]

It is difficult to imagine how this hymn would provide any knowledge of work previously inaccessible to future housewives. Certainly housework falls within the already familiar domestic sphere rather than without. The view of work presented here—the preparation of household items and food under the watchful eyes of God—neither serves to fill in the gaps in women's education nor represents a broadened perspective. The same could be said of the emphasis on the students' futures as wives.

Also included in the "Trabajo" section is Pablo Neruda's "Maestranzas de Noche [Foundries at Night]" from his first book of poetry, *Crepusculario* (1923). With no contextualization or explanation, the poem stands in stark contrast to the school hymn as a commentary on work outside the domestic sphere:

Black iron sleeping, black iron moaning
a sorrowing cry from every pore.

Spent ashes upon the sad earth,
thick broths where bronze was fused with pain.

From what far and unfortunate country,
these birds, croaking through endless nights of pain?

And the cry convulses me like a twisted nerve
or the broken string of a violin.

Each machine has its open eye
to stare at me.

Great question marks hang on the walls,
the soul of the bronze blooms upon anvils,
and there is a trembling of footsteps in the empty rooms.

And in desperation through the black night
the souls of dead workers run and sob.[36]

Her inclusion of "Foundries at Night" reveals Mistral's attitude toward the industrial. While housework, the creative arts, and pre-modern labor such as bricklaying and carpentry are glorified in the school's hymn and elsewhere in this section of the *Lecturas,* work that takes place in an industrial setting is characterized as menacing—"Each machine has its open eye / to stare at me"—and possibly fatal—"the souls of dead workers run and sob." Again we find Mistral rejecting the modern, which is in this case represented by the foundry. Neruda's poem is the only piece in the section to suggest a negative view of "work." In fact, the opening essay by Eugenio D'Ors, "El desdén del oficio (103)," is an argument for loving one's job, no matter how lowly and/or low-paying it may be.

Mistral's uneasiness with modernization/industrialization is apparent throughout the *Lecturas.* To return to the question posed earlier as to what is revealed by Mistral's opening a textbook directed toward women in postrevolutionary Mexico with such an anachronistic piece as Ruskin's speech from *Sesame and Lilies,* we have seen that her choice signals her ambiguous position. While Mistral's participation in the founding of the homemakers' schools and the writing of the *Lecturas* indicate her belief that women should be formally educated, women's "work" is presented as most valuable and wholesome when they operate within the domestic sphere. Despite the fact that the domestic—associated with women—is both tied and implicitly subordinate to the public—associated with men (remember the refrain of the hymn, "we are nurseries of wives")—Mistral ignores the relationship, let alone the imbalance, between those spheres and focuses instead on her idealized version of the realm of the *hogar* and, at its center, the *mujer antigua.* As a result, the *hogar* is separated from the external economic, political, and other forces by which it is shaped.

A deliberate move away from the public and away from female/male relationships surfaces in the both the "México y la América española" and "Naturaleza" sections of the *Lecturas,* which are quite similar in their themes. Though it does include some texts one might expect to find, such as writings by Vasconcelos and Martí about Cuauhtémoc and Hidalgo respectively, "México y la América española" also contains Mistral's essay "Croquis Mexicanos" (divided into the sections "El órgano," "El maguey," and "La palma real") as well as selections by other authors titled "La tortuga," "El girasol," "El maíz," "El venado y el faisán," and other ahistorical, apolitical, nature-oriented pieces. The inclusion of such texts in this section of the anthology would not be so striking were there not also a separate "Naturaleza" section. These escapes into nature seem to be more appropriate in that section, yet they appear amongst the few essays on historico-political figures.

In order to understand why Mistral makes such curious editorial choices, we might look to her poetry to give us some insight into her views on history. In her essay "Women, Literature, and National Brotherhood," Mary Louise Pratt observes that in the posthumously published *Poema de Chile,* Mistral takes a view of history that excludes the human world and events by focusing on nature: "Historicity is thus present in the *Poema de Chile* not in the form of canonical history (battles, treaties, dates to be commemorated) but in the 'micropractices' of social reproduction through which one generation continually shapes the next" (69). Pratt alludes here to the mother-child relationship between the poetic "I" and the adoptive indigenous child who accompanies her through Chile in the collection and to whom many of its individual poems are addressed. The *Poema* does refer to the nation, Chile, but the public world of politics and history is absent. Though the action of the poems takes place outside the physical boundaries of the home, the mother and child figures do not engage with the public world. They exist in a space apart from other humans (including a father) in which "the hills tell stories / and the houses little or nothing." As Pratt maintains, the mother's preference for the stories of hills signals an unwillingness on the poet's part to link history with the human world. On the other hand, she also identifies a hatred of houses as a recurrent theme in the *Poema* through which Mistral challenges the identification of women with the domestic (70). The *Poema* reveals an ambivalence about women's association with the home.

Mistral's approach to history in the *Poema* is similar to that of her contemporary, Teresa de la Parra, in *Las memorias de Mamá Blanca* (1929). In de la Parra's novel, women thrive in the ahistorical, apolitical setting of a nineteenth-century Venezuelan plantation. The protagonist, Blanca Nieves, and her five sisters move within a self-contained feminine universe in apparent isolation from Venezuelan reality. Though the novel is set after Independence, the world it evokes corresponds to de la Parra's interpretation of the colonial period which she characterizes as "[i]ngenuous and happy like children and like the towns that have no history. . . . Denuded of politics, of press, of wars, of industries, and of business, it is the long vacation of the men and the reign with neither chronicles nor chroniclers of the women."[37] The erasure of historical and material reality implicit in this approach has its obvious pitfalls, particularly in terms of its concealment or distortion of real social power relations such as those between husbands and wives or those between masters and slaves.[38] Like de la Parra's novel, Mistral's *Poema* both avoids the subjects of human history and politics and reveals the racial hierarchy implied in the relations it describes. Mistral's Euro-American poetic voice provides knowledge for the infantilized, dependent Indian (Pratt 70).

Still, both Mistral and de la Parra preferred their version of the past to what they saw as the present status of woman within the modern nation. To them, the past appeared relatively more expansive and free. Rather than confront the problems generated by a masculine "horizontal comradeship" in relation to the modern and the urban, they rejected the industrial world over which women appear to lack control.[39] In "Loca y no loca. La cultura popular en la obra de Gabriela Mistral," Jean Franco reads Mistral's recourse to oral traditions in her poetry as "an escape from the modernizing project of her time that, on the other hand, animated her pedagogical work" (29). Though the *Lecturas* are part of her pedagogical project, I would argue that they, like much of Mistral's poetry, favor a pre-modern or anti-modern space.

Pratt elaborates on Mistral's view of the past in a comparative reading of Rómulo Gallegos's *Doña Bárbara* and de la Parra's *Las memorias de Mamá Blanca*:

> [B]oth Mamá Blanca and Doña Bárbara stand for preindustrial social structures inherited from the colonial period and now seen to be passing. Both represent forms of female power and entitlement destroyed by modernization. Both remind us that, from a purely socioeconomic standpoint, the development of urban centers of power and elaborate state apparatuses threatened to deprive women heirs and property owners of an economic base for which there was no urban or industrial equivalent. (58)

In the *Lecturas,* Mistral does not refer specifically to the American colonial past as these authors do. As we have seen, the only concrete reference she makes to the past is to ancient Greece and Rome.

Just as she does in the *Poema de Chile*, Mistral avoids the question of the nation in the "México y la América española" section of the *Lecturas*. And her speech, "A la mujer mexicana," included there provides yet another example of her unease with women's place in the urban, the industrial, the modern world. The speech glorifies the mothers of old whom Mistral, like de la Parra, sees as relatively more empowered. In an extremely rare reference to contemporary social problems, however, "A la mujer mexicana" also encourages women to ask the government for changes that will improve their children's lives:

> Ask for his sake for the sunny and clean school, ask for the happy parks; ask for the feasts of images, in books and in instructive cinema; demand to collaborate on laws, but when dealing with the things that defile you or diminish your life, you can ask for laws that wipe the shame from the illegitimate child who is made to be born a pariah and live a pariah in the midst of the other children, and laws that regulate your work and that of the children who exhaust themselves in the brutal labor of the factories.[40]

Though, as we have seen, Mistral's conservative views on women's education put her at odds with some of her feminist contemporaries, her mention of children's rights—albeit brief in the context of the whole anthology—aligns Mistral with Latin American women's organizations that have historically demanded rights and protections in areas pertaining to the traditional roles of wife and mother.[41] What is characteristic is Mistral's mistrust of the modern industrial world. Her description of factory work as "brutal" refers to the dehumanizing effects of unregulated industrial labor. The appeal to the rights of children represents another avenue by which Mistral attacks the patriarchal formation of the nation.

The closing passages of this speech are an indication of Mistral's aversion to nationalism and gravitation toward an internationalism that she also shares with most Latin American feminist groups: "Our race will prove itself in your children; in them we must save ourselves or perish. God fixed upon them the hard fate that the waves of the North should break upon their chest. For this reason, when your children struggle or sing, the faces of the South turn this way full of both hope and disquiet."[42] Here again, Mistral does not address the role of wife as much as she does the role of mother. The absence of men in both the speech and the anthology becomes very apparent when we consider her above remarks on the "illegitimate child." By her specific mention of the stigma of illegitimacy, Mistral evokes the perceived threat to male hegemony posed by women who bear children outside the control of the legal institution of marriage. Her views on this subject as they are expressed in "A la mujer mexicana" are radical in relation to the other claims she urges Mexican women to make. They are par-

ticularly vexing when we consider the anxiety the issue of illegitimacy provokes in a society whose founding myths involve *la Malinche,* the unwed
mother of Mexican mestizo identity.

Though she begins with a call to women as reproducers of the national
citizen — "your belly sustains the race; the citizen multitudes are born quietly of your womb" — she goes on to associate the nation with nature,
"beautiful and strong is the land to which it fell to you to be born, Mexican
mother: it has the most perfect fruits in the world and turns out the softest
and most delightful tufts of cotton," and then links mothers with nature,
"You are *the collaborator of the earth* and so she bathes you with grace in
the light of each morning."[43] By the time Mistral directs herself to illegitimacy she has travelled through nation, nature, motherhood: a path which
allows her to skirt traditional nationalist rhetoric. Her mention of illegitimacy is in keeping with the woman-centered world she imagines and
is resistant to the concept of the nation as brotherhood, for as Pratt notes,
"the reproductive capacity so indispensable to the brotherhood [the nation]
is a source of peril, notably in the capacity of those nonfinite, all-too-elastic
female bodies to reproduce themselves outside the control of the frater-
nity. It was no accident that modern nations denied full citizens' rights to
illegitimate offspring, and that women's political platforms continuously
demanded those rights" (52). Despite her exaltation of the traditional
mother-child bond, we can read Mistral's sidestepping of the traditional
historico-political definition of the nation as a rejection of the role prescribed for women within that imagined space. As we have seen, the gesture
is contradictory since it is characterized by both resistance and conformity;
her reach beyond nationalism and the public sphere employs traditional
patriarchal conceptions of women's roles.

When Mistral urges her audience in "A la mujer mexicana" to reject the
example of modern women, her use of the phrase "mujeres locas del siglo"
(crazy women of this century) prefigures images of the women appearing in
"Locas mujeres," the first section of *Lagar* (1954). Little critical attention
has been paid to these poems, though it has been suggested that they might
be read as self-portraits of their author.[44] Mistral's critics have not refrained
from reading the poet's life into her works. In fact, certain biographically
oriented readings of her more widely read poetry have helped to create and
to perpetuate the myths surrounding Mistral and her writings.

In *Gabriela Mistral: The Poet and Her Work,* the first biography to appear after Mistral's death, Margot Arce de Vázquez posits direct connections between the poet's personal life and the thematic content of her writings:

Shortly after this first literary triumph [winning the poetic Floral Games in Santiago in 1914], she met under romantic and somewhat strange circumstances a young poet from Santiago; for him she felt a passion much deeper, more intense and more decisive than her first love. A short while later, however, he married a wealthy young lady of the capital's high social circles. The cruel blow moved her to ask for her transfer to Punta Arenas in the extreme south of Chile, an inhospitable, desolate region [. . .] The most moving and impassioned poems of *Desolación,* the very title of that anguished book, express with ardent eloquence her heartbreaking disillusion. She turned her gaze to children and wrote for them, transforming her frustrated longing for motherhood into tenderness. In her affection for the American lands and peoples and in the pleasures of friendship she sought the companionship denied to her by love. (4–5)

These assertions, made in a section of the biography titled "Emotional Life," are typical of characterizations of Mistral as an artist who, unable to realize her true love, loved "America" instead. By extension, she is seen to sublimate her desire to be a mother into concern for children in general. The central themes of Mistral's writings are understood to have arisen from her tragically unfulfilled desires for physical love and childbearing. In this case, the fact that her biographer declines to name the man directly responsible for so much of Mistral's poetic production and that their meeting is described as "romantic and somewhat strange" only adds drama and mystery to the myth.

While this characterization robs Mistral of her agency by suggesting that her writing is a response to some unfulfilled feminine instinct, other biographical elements provided by Arce de Vázquez suggest cracks in the myth. We learn, for example, that Mistral became known early in her career for her "anti-bourgeois social ideas" (5). We find that the chaplain of a normal school rejected Mistral's application because she had published newspaper articles expounding socialist philosophy and that later in life, Mistral published anti-fascist essays that caused Mussolini to block her appointment as Chile's Consul to Italy (2, 8). Arce de Vázquez's biography also reveals that Mistral was corresponding with internationally known authors, including the Mexican poet Amado Nervo, and that she received encouragement from Pedro Aguirre la Cerda, who later became the president of Chile (3). The political views and connections to men with public careers revealed in these and other biographical moments conflict with the private, domestic, maternal image of Mistral that the biographer tries to cast. The patriarchal endorsements that Mistral herself worked for both in and outside Chile combine ideally with the conservative ideology of the male Mexican revolutionaries at whose invitation she goes to Mexico to participate in Vasconcelos's educational reform. It is worth remembering that Mistral was invited by Vasconcelos to come to Mexico as a pedagogue and outstanding figure in Latin American letters in 1922. To that point, she had not published one book. Only in that year, 1922, was her first book of poetry, *Desolación*, published in New York.

Arce de Vázquez appears unsure about the public acclaim Mistral achieved: "She also began to win fame abroad, both for the writings she published in the press and for the correspondence she carried on with notable Hispanic-American writers, among them Rubén Darío himself" (5). The biographer seems surprised that Mistral should correspond with such a famous writer. Her doubts are likewise revealed by the way she discusses the Nobel Prize: "Perhaps it was the profound value of her poetry as a work of art and as a human document and of her prose as an expression of values essential to contemporary man that won for her the highest literary award in the world" (7). The uncertainty Arce de Vázquez expresses as to why Mistral won the prize marks the limits of viewing Mistral as the quintessentially "feminine." Perhaps the lovelorn and private poet Arce de Vázquez has constructed is incompatible with someone capable of qualifying for such a prestigious, public prize. Similarly, this portrait stands at odds with the ambition evident in Mistral's career as poet and public figure.

The title of Volodia Teitelboim's more recent biography, *Gabriela Mistral pública y secreta: Truenos y silencios en la vida del primer Nobel latinoamericano* [Public and secret Gabriela Mistral: thunders and silences in the life of the first Latin American Nobel] (1991), suggests that his work addresses some of the mystery and the myths in which Mistral's image has been cloaked. Teitelboim's approach differs from Vázquez's in that he is quite conscious of the myths. Of the "official legend" that grew out of the suicide of Romelio Ureta, the supposed inspiration for Mistral's *Sonetos de la muerte*, he writes:

> Often [Mistral] would give mistaken versions, perfectly capable of letting a story that would suggest wrong turns run along the surface. At times the alibi was turned into truth, repeated generation after generation . . . Upon writing "Los sonetos de la muerte" she herself generates the fiction colored by tragedy. She converts a marginal epi-

sode into the spark that makes the fire spread in the forest. She literarily creates a myth that grows and exalts the imagination of the readers.[45]

Unlike Arce de Vázquez, Teitelboim names the person involved in the relationship, acknowledges the myth, and also suggests that Mistral allowed the myth to be perpetuated.[46] While taking the mystery out of this particular "love story," Teitelboim's overall treatment does not significantly rework Mistral's image. Nor does it suggest why she might have encouraged the myth herself. This biographer substitutes one mythic relationship for another by suggesting that it was actually another man, Alberto Pineda, who inspired Mistral's writing: "Who was that 'impossible love?' Did he exist? Cinderella's blue prince did exist. He was rich, handsome."[47] Here we have the same drama, a different man.

In the midst of his accounts of Mistral's romances, enclosed between his versions of the Pineda and Ureta stories, Teitelboim curiously includes a section titled "¡Honor a los que se acuerdan de la mujer!" He argues that one could write an entire book titled "Gabriela Mistral and the Woman": "She was always passionate about the subject, to the limits of obsession, because, at the bottom of it, when she touched on it she was touching on herself."[48] He relates this "obsession" to what he considers to be Mistral's incredible memory for her sufferings: "She was dominated by a tenacious memory, timeproof, indelible for derision and contempt. She lived possessed by aversions without remission and by perpetual taboos."[49]

Among Mistral's aversions is one to the institution of marriage, against which she "declared war" in a newspaper article published when she was seventeen (37). Teitelboim connects Mistral's objection to marriage, her aversions and taboos, and her passion for the subject of "the woman" by suggesting that they are a product of her failed relationships with men.[50] As in Arce de Vázquez's account, there is an intermingling here of Mistral's supposed romantic relationships and her career. What neither critic addresses is Mistral's lesbianism. When Teitelboim states that Mistral enjoyed the women's rights meetings that she, "the abandoned young teacher" (38), began to attend after her break with Pineda, we are led to read the adjective *abandonada* both in terms of her difficult teaching career and in terms of relationships with men. Despite the importance of "the woman" that Teitelboim himself acknowledges in Mistral's life, he continues to look to her relationships with men as the inspiration for her poetry. In this 1991 biography then, the Mistralian myths, though modified and somewhat less mysterious, remain intact. Any allusion to lesbian relationships remains unspoken.[51]

Palma Guillén de Nicolau approaches the myths in her 1976 introduction to the Porrúa collected edition of *Desolación—Ternura—Tala—Lagar*. She too asserts that Mistral encouraged the development of a romantic myth about her one lost love as the subject of all of her love poetry: "Did she do it to create or to affirm the romantic myth of the woman with only one true love? . . . I must honestly say that I do not know why she did it. I tell myself, to understand, that maybe she wanted to mix the various men with those she loved because in them she looked for one whom she did not find."[52] As a companion of Mistral for several years, Guillén de Nicolau may be quietly suggesting room for herself amongst the subjects of Mistral's poems. This is certainly not an unlikely assertion given that Mistral dedicated her book *Tala* to her.

Guillén de Nicolau finishes her introduction to the collected poems by calling the reader's attention to what she terms "'self-portraits' in which the true Gabriela, the Gabriela of flesh and bones, shows her face—her child's face, her youth's face, her woman's face—in her poetry."[53] Though mediated forms of expression, these poems may shed different light on Mistral's thoughts and on her strategy of deflecting attention away from her person in her prose writings. Among these illuminating texts are all of the poems in "Locas mujeres."

The poem that Guillén de Nicolau considers to be the most complete self-portrait of Mistral is "La otra," in which the poetic voice kills a part of herself: "I killed someone inside myself: / I didn't love her."[54] *La otra* is described as dryness and fire: "She had rock and sky / at her feet and her back / and she never went down / to look for 'eyes of water'. // Where she napped, / the plants coiled up / from the heat of her breath / and the coals of her face."[55] Though she characterizes her *otra* as inflexible, scorching, harsh, the poem's speaker is unforgiving in her own right, stealing the entrails from her other and leaving *la otra* to wither and die: "She didn't know how to bend / the mountain plant; / and at her side, I bent . . . // I let her die, stealing my entrails from her. / She ended like the eagle / who isn't fed."[56] Still, the end of the poem suggests that *la otra* in some way lives on. As her sisters cry out at her loss, the travelling speaker responds, "—Search in the ravines / and make with clay / another flaming eagle. // If you cannot, then, / oh!, forget her. / I killed her. You / too should kill her!"[57] Guillén de Nicolau argues that the female voice killed in this poem is the one who suffers in Mistral's painful poetry, and especially in the poems of *Desolación* (xxxix).[58] Not surprisingly, *Desolación* contains the "Sonetos de la muerte" which inspired critics to focus so relentlessly on the loss of Mistral's heterosexual "true love."

Titles of the "Locas mujeres" poems suggest their tones and themes: "La otra," "La abandonada," "La ansiosa," "La desasida," "La desvelada," "La fervorosa," "La fugitiva," "La que camina." Though Mistral was known as the "spiritual mother" of Latin America, no mother figures appear in these portraits. Rather, most of the female subjects of "Locas mujeres" are lone(ly) wandering women. Often they are angry as is *la abandonada*: "Give me now the words / that my wet nurse did not give to me / I will babble them demented / syllable by syllable: / word 'despoil,' word 'nothing' / and word 'twilight,' / though they twist in my mouth / like wasted vipers!"[59] The words the wet nurse did not give her, and which she now demands, all focus on endings, on emptiness, on absence. Her betrayal leads her to demand from the auditor the words which will allow her to express her sense of abandonment. *La abandonada* deliberately destroys all that she and the "you" to whom she addresses herself once had:

> I'm burning all that we had:
> the thick walls, the high beams,
> liquidating one by one
> the twelve doors that you opened
> and clogging with hatchet blows
> the well of happiness.
> I'm going to spread, scattered,
> the harvest picked yesterday,
> and empty the wineskins
> and free captive birds;
> and break like my body
> the members of the 'masía'
> and measure with tall arms
> the heap of the ashes.[60]

Their house, their crops, their animals, their wine, the entire domestic scene and the relationship for which it serves as a metaphor are ripped up, clogged, hatcheted, scattered, poured out, and consumed in a burning revenge. *La abandonada* seems to revel in her act of revenge, of striking out against the betrayal she has endured. The image of domesticity here is one of conflict and unfulfillment, of absence and discontinuity. Such imagery hardly evokes a scene of domestic bliss like those prescribed in the *Lecturas*.

Mistral's poem "Electra in the Mist" also represents a striking contrast to images of motherhood portrayed in the *Lecturas*. In this poetic reworking of the classical myth, Electra claims responsibility for the murder of her mother, Clytemnestra. Walking through a sea mist, she talks to herself : "I walk free not hearing her cry / come back to me, not hearing her voices, / for she no longer walks, she now lies still. / And her words flutter in vain around her, / and her gestures, her name, her laugh, / while I and Orestes walk / the Attic lands of Hellas, hers and ours (134). At this point, Electra believes she has freed herself from the mother who does not love her: "Only Iphigenia and her lover did she love / in the narrowness of her cold breast. / Me and Orestes she left without a kiss, / without her fingers intertwined in ours" (134). Again, the nurturing breast fails to supply what the speaker needs. Where the wet nurse's breast could not supply the words for the speaker in "La abandonada" to express herself, here Clytemnestra's breasts are narrow and cold. The daughter strikes back against the betraying mother in order to avenge the unjust murder of her father. As she wanders by the sea, Electra realizes a new identity which she articulates at the opening of the poem: "Now, I am just the one who killed" (133). After her extended meditation on her actions, Electra comes to see that she has not rid herself of Clytemnestra. In death, the betraying mother has now spread everywhere: "But it is she who passes, not the mist. / She who was one, and in one palace, / is now mist-albatross, mist-road, / mist-sea, mist-hamlet, and mist-ship" (136). As mist, Clytemnestra engulfs the hapless and helpless daughter. The betraying—not the nurturing—mother haunts the murdering daughter.

These poems offer a vision that betrays the myth of woman as nurturing mother. It would appear that in her poetic expression Mistral does not feel as compelled to conform to patriarchal convention as she does in her prose work. In part, this must be attributable to the public nature of the *Lecturas* as they are linked to a nationalist cultural project. However, as we have seen, even within the *Lecturas* contradictions appear as Mistral both encourages women to reproduce the national citizenry and deflects the impossible role women are to play within the modern nation.

This impossible role Mistral herself plays. Portrayed as the Mother of Latin America, Mistral used the image of nurturer and caretaker to deflect more pressing issues of personal identity. There is no denying that Mistral at times encouraged a stereotyped view of herself despite its dissonance with her public/professional career as ambassador and pedagogue. This was perhaps the logical outcome of her disjunctive traditional approach to women's roles. It follows too, then, that she would deny her role as literary and cultural critic. Mistral wrote hundreds of newspaper and magazine articles and several lengthy book prologues. Much of this literary criticism is found in what she called her *"recados,"* or *"cartas para muchos,"* published in various Latin American newspapers and journals. Despite the volume and intensity of her critical work, Mistral did not consider herself a literary critic.

We might, in closing, consider the dissonance between what Mistral says in *Lecturas para mujeres* and what she in fact does. She advises women to remain in the private sphere of the domestic as giver and carer of life. The role she ascribes for them neatly inserts nationalist interests into the domestic space. She herself, however, throughout most of her life worked outside the home in the public sphere. As Jean Franco observes, "the public persona cultivated by Mistral not only permitted her to occupy an exceptional space, transforming herself into a symbol, but also to hide under a mask of maternity, the fact that she did not conform to heterosexuality and the reproductive role for women promoted by the State" ("Loca" 28–29).

The discontinuity of Mistral's practices and her theories reveals the alienation of women from the public sphere. They are largely excluded from roles that might directly alter this male-dominated space. Mistral's life and works embody what Francine Masiello describes as "the displacement or homelessness of the female intellectual" ("Women" 37). Unlike the women to whom Masiello refers (Teresa de la Parra, María Luisa Bombal, Norah Lange), Mistral did not fully refuse "the unifying discourse that maintains the female body in place, limiting woman to reproductive functions or domestic labor" (37). What she refused for herself personally she advocates in her public and conflicted writings for and about women.

AFTERWORD

I began this book by calling attention to the exclusion of Latin American women from literary/cultural institutions. I went on to articulate some of the strategies employed by three particular women to produce cultural knowledge in the face of that exclusion. In doing so, I have drawn extensively on the growing body of research by present-day scholars—almost all of them women—who dedicate themselves to broadening our understanding of women as social and cultural actors through their teaching and publishing. Without their efforts, mine would not be possible.

From the perspective of the end of the twentieth century, I have examined the problems of reception and interpretation of the works of these early-twentieth-century writers and thereby provided one way of rethinking the structuration of Latin American literary criticism. Moving between their creative writings and their own literary critical endeavors, I have examined the ways in which they engaged in important cultural debates of the early twentieth century, particularly those involving the definition of "the national." Their stories teach us about the relations between Third World women intellectuals and the materials of representation in critical discourse and creative writing.

I have centered my discussion of each writer on what I perceive as a central contradiction. Lúcia Miguel Pereira omits women from her critical texts though her novels comprise a series of female *bildungsromane*. Within her literary criticism, gendered analysis is displaced by and sublimated through her representations of race. Victoria Ocampo's writing is often cast as too personal and therefore devalued. Tellingly, the work of many of her male peers, though often similar in form, is not similarly dismissed. I have attempted to show the ways in which Ocampo's work concerns itself with the *personal as public* and how it is indeed inserted into the larger questions of cultural nationalism. Her writings force us to rethink the relationship between the private and the public, between feminine and masculine representivity. Finally, the case of the most famous figure of the three— perhaps the best-known Latin American woman writer of the twentieth century—is also the most fraught with contradiction. The received image of Gabriela Mistral is that of a spiritual mother of the Americas. A substantial volume of criticism that explains her poetry as a lament to spinsterhood has developed around this maternal mythology. While Mistral does highlight traditional women's roles in much of her writing, she radicalizes the significance of those roles in relation to the national space, forging a domestic utopia as an act of resistance to homogenizing modernity. Domestic space, however, is always impinged upon by masculinist, heterosexist discourses about its significance.

Despite the differing positions they occupy within Latin American literary history, the writings of all three women underscore how embedded they are in the dominant discourses on culture of the early twentieth century. All of them valorize in some form or another European standards of judgment. Miguel Pereira works to define the Brazilian literary tradition, but always within the framework of European cultural values. Ocampo calls for the building of bridges between the Americas and Europe, yet her views reveal her sense of the superiority that European culture represents. Mistral sings the praises of Latin America while holding up classical Greek and Roman culture as the standard by which it should be judged. In these ways, their work speaks to the position of Latin America as a colonized cultural space. Their writings are thus informed by tensions and conflicts evident throughout Latin America as its intellectuals wrestle with the relationship between their national cultures and the dominant world powers.

Much can be learned from the struggles and failures of each of these women's careers. In an active rejection of the notion that women have not engaged in the production of culture and knowledge, more investigation needs to be undertaken that examines the ways in which women did and do engage with the very *public* issues from which their relegation to the *private* supposedly precludes them.

NOTES

Chapter One. The Bearded Academy

1. Unlike Sarmiento and Juárez, Floresta (Nísia Floresta Brasileira Augusta) held no government post, and it is difficult to measure her influence on Brazil's educational system. According to Norma Telles, Floresta's newspaper articles published in Rio provoked polemics (405). We do have evidence that her translation into Portuguese of Mary Wollstonecraft's *A Vindication of the Rights of Woman* (in its third edition in 1839) did not go unnoticed. The protagonist in Manuel Macedo's novel *A moreninha* (1844) is mocked for reading it. See Sharpe's "Brazilian Women and Social Reform in Nísia Floresta's *Opúsculo*" and her "Nísia Floresta: *Woman*" for further information on Floresta.

2. See Lavrin for further information on women in Argentina, Chile, and Uruguay at the turn of the century.

3. The first woman known to be involved in print journalism in Latin America is Señora de Bernardo Calderón, whose name appeared on a news sheet in Mexico in 1684 (Seminar 173–174). Unless otherwise noted, all intertextual references will refer to the list of works cited, located at the end of this book.

4. I mention Mexico in the case of Mistral because *Lecturas para mujeres*, the central focus of chapter four, was written under the aegis of the Mexican government.

5. This and all further translations are mine unless otherwise indicated. Doris Sommer extrapolates from Bello's view: "narrative becomes necessary, not only because the gaps in our historical knowledge make more 'modern' methods unfeasible, but also because the filler can be taken for an origin of independent and local expression" (9).

6. The novel *Soledad*, with its manifesto/prologue, was published in 1847.

7. See Foucault's "What Is an Author?" for his explanation of the "author function." Foucault does not develop his argument in terms of gender.

8. One of the best-known case studies of gender-marking and the reception of a literary text is Carol Ohmann's "Emily Brontë in the Hands of Male Critics," in which

she compares reviews of *Wuthering Heights*. Reviewers who assumed that its author was a man praised the novel for its power and originality. One went so far as to imagine the rough-sailor type the author must have been (908). Reviews in which the author was identified as a woman focused on her life. Another likened her to "a little bird fluttering its wings against the bars of its cage, only to sink at the last, exhausted" (909). Ohmann concludes that there is a strong correlation between what readers see/ignore in a text and their presuppositions about the sex of its author.

9. See Sylvia Molloy's discussion of autobiography, biography, and history in chapter eight of her *At Face Value: Autobiographical Writing in Spanish America*.

10. "El nombre que se ha dado a la obra entera, se explica por su contenido. Un destino cometa, que de pronto refulge, luego se apaga en largos trechos de sombra, y el ambiente turbio del México actual, justifican la analogía con la clásica *Odisea*" (6). English translation from Molloy (*At Face Value* 190).

11. See chapter three for a more detailed discussion of this process in the cases of Victoria Ocampo and Roberto Giusti.

12. "Ha tendido los brazos, y ha abarcado con ellos el secreto de la vida. De su cuerpo, cestilla ligera de su alado espíritu, ascendió entre labores dolorosas y mortales ansias, a esas cúspides puras, desde donde se dibujan, como en premio el afán del viajador las túnicas bordadas de luz estelar de los seres infinitos. Ha sentido ese desborde misterioso del alma en el cuerpo, que es ventura solemne, y llena los labios de besos, y las manos de caricias, y los ojos de llanto, y se parece al súbito hinchamiento y rebose de la Naturaleza en primavera." (Martí 12)

13. I am indebted to Chela Sandoval for calling my attention to Castillo's reference to "the great white mother" of feminist literary criticism.

14. "We see collective practice as the key to our efforts to mediate among literary studies, history, politics, area studies, feminist theory, and Europe and the Americas" (viii).

15. In "Latin American Feminism and the Transnational Arena," Miller focuses on the proceedings of inter-American conferences held between 1880 and 1948 among which were the Latin American Scientific Congresses (Buenos Aires 1898, Montevideo 1901, Rio de Janeiro 1905); the Pan American Scientific Congresses (Santiago 1908, Washington, D.C. 1915–1916); the Congreso Femenino Internacional (Buenos Aires 1910); the Pan American Conference of Women (Baltimore 1922); the meetings of the Inter-American Commission of Women (Havana 1930, Lima 1938); and the Congreso Interamericano de Mujeres (Guatemala City 1947).

16. See, for example, *Historia de la literatura mexicana desde los orígenes hasta nuestros días* by Carlos González Peña (1928), *Historia de la literatura argentina* by Ricardo Rojas (1917 [1960]), and *Noções da história da literatura brasileira* (1931) by Afrânio Peixoto. Biographies include Lúcia Miguel Pereira's *Vida de Gonçalves Dias* and *Machado de Assis,* discussed below.

17. See volume 8, chapter 17 ("Las mujeres escritoras") of Ricardo Rojas's *Historia de la literatura argentina* (first published as *La literatura argentina; ensayo filosófico sobre la evolución de la cultura en el Plata* in 1917) and José Toribio Medina's *La literatura femenina en Chile* (1923) for examples of how women intellectuals of the nineteenth century are incorporated into national literary histories.

18. "Todas aquellas disciplinas estudian la literatura como instrumento, como problema, como parte de la cultura general, pero dejan algo sin tocar: el juicio de valor. Nadie, si no la crítica, arremete por este lado. La crítica juzga si una obra es o no literatura; juzga la excelencia literaria de un a obra; juzga la jerarquía de su valor. Lo que la crítica tiene que decirnos lo puede decir en muy pocas palabras: 'esto vale, esto no vale'." (27)

19. Translation by Nina M. Scott in D. Meyer (36).

20. For an extensive discussion of person, authority, and critical authorship from the perspective of a contemporary North American academic, see Nancy Miller's *Getting Personal: Feminist Occasions and Other Autobiographical Acts*. Her first chapter, "Autobiography as Cultural Criticism," engages with current debates on "personal criticism."

Chapter Two. Lúcia Miguel Pereira and the Era(c)ing of Brazilian National Literature

1. Because Brazilian orthography has officially changed since the novels were published, I have modified the Portuguese in quotations and titles throughout this discussion with the exception of the proper name and title *Maria Luiza*.

2. "meninas, antes querem-se pouco instruídas do que vagando a sós pelas ruas" (37).

3. "Não podia acreditar honestas mulheres que cuidassem de alguma coisa além da casa e dos filhos. Confundia, na mesma condenação sumária e inflexível, as elegantes e as intelectuais" (69).

4. "acordavam nela uma mulher desconhecida, revoltada contra a mesmice da vida, vibrante de loucas aspirações" (148).

5. "Em frases curtas, marteladas e ardentes, disse o seu horror pela educação que recebera; o crime de fabricarem os pais um mundo imaginário para as filhas, que tarde ou cedo descobrirão o engano de que foram vítimas" (166).

6. "Naturalmente, se ele fizesse a loucura de se querer casar, esbarraria como Jorge nalguma tolinha que lhe preferiria um doutor sem eira nem beira. Casar . . . aguentar uma familia . . . Brrr . . . Que horror! Nenhuma mulher valia a sua liberdade; se podia tê-las, quantas quisesse, sem sacrificar coisa alguma. . . ." (27).

7. "Era feita de migalhas da existência dos outros? Não importava, se com essas migalhas, com essas sobras, ela conseguira construir a sua" (364).

8. "Se fosse ele que tivesse morrido, e mamãe houvesse vivido como ele o fêz, seria uma mulher desonesta. Admitindo a correção dele, você tem também de admitir uma moral diferente para cada sexo, o que implica o completo artificialismo da moral" (363).

9. "O meu noivo seria . . . estudante de medicina, e eu teria criadas, vestidos bonitos, leria romances sentada numa poltrona" (8).

10. "Disse-me que seguisse o seu exemplo, que não contasse com ninguém, que lutasse, que trabalhasse. Eu não podia viver de esmolas, nem me enterrar viva em São José. Não podia também esperar do céu um príncipe encantado" (89–90).

11. "eu serei sua amante, Antônio, sua criada, sua escrava" (213).

12. "Eu só me sinto bem na companhia de pessoas assim, que me ofusquem um

pouco. Antônio costuma dizer que eu tenho necessidade de me humilhar e sustenta que há em mim um fundo de sadismo" (222).

13. "A virgindade—como me envergonhou ouvir dele essa palavra!—o casamento eram preconceitos. Preconceito burguês, a noção de honra feminina. O prazer é desfrutado tanto pela moça como pelo rapaz; não há culpa para aquela nem responsabilidade para este. Deviam ser dois parceiros, não emprestando gravidade a coisas que não a tinham. O amor era muito raro, e o instinto muito premente. Por que ligar um ao outro? Daí provinham os recalques sexuais, de consequências funestas. Disse isso e muita coisa mais. Mas para mim, isso tudo só significava que ele não gostava de mim. *Recompuz-lhe as idéias mais porque o ouvi repeti-las muitas vezes, depois, do que pelo que entendi no momento.*" (70–71)

14. "o crime de fabricarem os pais um mundo imaginário para as filhas, que tarde ou cedo descobrirão o engano de que foram vítimas" (166).

15. "Chegar em casa tendo vindo do apartamento de um desconhecido será uma vingança íntima, mas completa, magnífica. Cada um não tem um segredo, até a avó? Pois também terá o seu" (202).

16. "Quem entrou para a Academia não foi eu, foi o povo do Ceará" (qtd. in Buarque de Hollanda 94).

17. The female poet Amélia Bevilacqua nominated herself in 1930. See Buarque de Hollanda's "A roupa da Rachel" for a brief history of women and the Brazilian Academy of Letters.

18. In addition to *O quinze,* her novels include *João Miguel* (1937), *Caminho de pedras* (1937), *As três Marias* (1939), and *Dora, Doralina* (1974). She has also published several plays, children's books, and countless short stories and *crônicas.*

19. "*O quinze* caiu de repente ali por meados de 30 e fez nos espíritos estragos maiores que o romance de José Américo, por ser livro de mulher e, o que realmente causava assombro, de mulher nova. Seria realmente de mulher? Não acreditei. Lido o volume e visto o retrato no jornal, balancei a cabeça: não há ninguém com este nome. É pilhéria. Uma garota assim fazer romance! Deve ser pseudônimo de sujeito barbado" (75).

20. "O romancista—que nisso se assemelha ao poeta, embora divirjam as reações— precisa receber a vida, deixar-se penetrar por ela, numa passividade propícia à gestação. Há alguma coisa de feminino na sua atitude, e de másculo na do crítico" (*Leitora* 127).

21. Though in later editions its title was *Prosa de ficção: de 1870 a 1920,* this study was first published in 1950 as volume 12 in the unfinished *História da literatura brasileira* edited by Álvaro Lins.

22. "[T]alvez, quando se estuda uma literatura ainda incipiente, como é o caso, se possa, e se deva, sem cair no historicismo, atribuir maior importância às circunstâncias do tempo e do meio" (17).

23. "E mesmo a uma ou outra lembrada pelos críticos do momento . . . não se pode dar lugar na história literária" (259).

24. I use the Spanish spelling of the word *mestizo* because it has entered American English.

25. "No caso da filiação de Machado de Assis, a paterna é infinitamente mais

importante do que a materna. O que o marcaria para sempre, o que condicionaria as suas reações diante dos homens e da vida, seria a cor que herdara do pai, e que a mãe pode ter atenuado, sem contudo deixar menos visível" (*Machado* 12).

26. "Depois de ter escrito um livro sobre Machado de Assis, assaltou-me . . . a tentação de fazer outro sobre Gonçalves Dias, de estudar o nosso primeiro grande poeta depois do nosso maior romancista, de reunir de algum modo esses dois mestiços admiráveis" (5).

27. The term *cafuza* refers to a person of both Native American and African descent.

28. "o seu temperamento se explica pela herança combinada das três raças—a portuguesa, do pai, a índia e a negra, da mãe" (13).

29. "nossos dois maiores romancistas mortos" (*Prosa* 277).

30. "para traduzir sua posição em face da vida" (*Prosa* 276).

31. "E as deficiências de que sofreram hão de ter aproximado o homem que escrevia 'escondendo o que sentia, para não se rebaixar' e o que o fazia 'com muito temor de não dizer tudo o que queria e sentia, sem calcular se se rebaixava ou se se exaltava.'

"Se não saiu, como Machado, da extrema pobreza, Lima Barreto era também mulato, e isso significa muito, infelizmente, nesta nossa paradoxal terra de mestiços; se não foi, como Machado, um completo autodidata, não pôde, chefe de família aos vinte e um anos, em virtude da doença paterna, terminar o curso que começara na Escola Politécnica; se não padeceu como Machado de moléstia nervosa, o seu alcoolismo—que há de estar ligado à loucura do pai—mais de uma vez o colocou à beira da insânia" (277).

32. "não por ser mestiço, mas por haver saído do povo, por ter pertencido a diferentes camadas sociais" (68).

33. "Não é impossível que no seu indianismo, tivesse entrado o íntimo impulso de se apegar ao índio, numa transposição, para o plano pessoal, do que se deu no plano nacional—o desejo de enaltecer uma raça de que se jactava, encobrindo o de fazer esquecer a outra, que o poderia humilhar" (16).

34. "A *inferioridade* racial, que pode compensar pelo orgulho do descendente dos primeiros donos da terra, lhe há de ter sido menos penosa do que a social, que só pelo seu valor próprio conseguiu contrabalançar" (7). It should be noted that Miguel Pereira does not qualify or contextualize the word "inferioridade."

35. "Além da mãe, só veria . . . os pretos das plantações de algodão e os índios mansos, fabricantes dos potes de barro usados em sua casa, com quem se foi familiarizando desde cedo" (20).

36. "Caxias devia ser mais roça do que cidade, cheia de negros, de matutos, de índios mansos . . . em bandos pelas ruas 'em completa nudez e selvajeria primitivas,' trocando com os habitantes 'peças de vestuário, machados, facas e toda espécie de ninharias' por 'grandes bolas de cera, plumas de belos coloridos e arcos e flechas delicadamente esculpidos.'

"Menino, Gonçalves Dias há-de ter brincado com esses instrumentos indígenas, há-de ter aprendido muita palavra dos selvagens que lhe eram familiares. Bebia água nos potes de barro por eles fabricados; via a mãe guardar em cuias e cabaças, umas lisas, outras bonitas, coloridas, os quitutes que preparava; dormia embalado nas redes de fibra ou de algodão, tão gostosas; via na cozinha o tipití indígena para fazer farinha. Ouviria certamente falar em Tapuais, em Timbiras, em Tupís, em guerras de índios; saberia povoados por eles as matas que avistava" (20–21). Miguel Pereira quotes J. B. von Spix and C. F. P. von Martius, *Viagem pelo Brasil*, trans. D. Lúcia Furquim Werneck (Rio: Instituto Histórico Geográfico Brasileiro, 1938).

37. "cortou violentamente as amarras com o passado . . . não querendo . . . ter constantemente diante dos olhos esse espectro de uma infância penosa, abandonou a pobre mulata," "Para subir de classe precisou sacrificar a madrastra" (*Machado* 123, 156).

38. "[a] própria pureza de língua do nosso maior prosador pode ter sofrido a influência do convívio com essa portuguesa cultivada" (*Machado* 119).

39. "Sem dúvida, generosa como era, Carolina não se teria recusado a receber em sua casa a mulata que fora tão boa para o seu querido Machado—se este lho houvesse pedido. Mas certamente foi ele quem preferiu a separação, e talvez mesmo houvesse ocultado da mulher a influência de Maria Inês na sua vida. Temeria a presença dessa nota dissonante na harmonia do seu interior. E, se, moralmente, andou mal, muito mal, psicologicamente acertou. Já não falando da humilhação constante que seria para ele essa prova irrefutável da sua origem modesta, como se poderiam entender as duas, a letrada Carolina e a humilde Maria Inês? Ambas ficariam constrangidas, e ele ainda mais do que elas" (156).

40. "qual o português que não se arranja, nos primeiros tempos, com as mulheres de cor? O tom pouco importa; negras, mulatas, ou acobreadas, todas servem, todas são submissas, carinhosas e econômicas—todas são mulheres e criadas" (22).

41. "Que faria ela, a pobre, do seu corpo quente de mestiça e da sua ternura de primitiva, se não arranjasse novo companheiro?" (22).

42. "[I]ria de vez em quando a São Cristóvão, onde deve ter ficado Maria Inês, reveria o antigo bairro, as ruas familiares, todos os testemunhos desse passado que queria enterrar, como um cadáver.

"Evocá-lo, era revolver uma chaga escondida, era trazer à consciência toda a amargura adormecida pelos triunfos recentes.

"À noite, depois das viagens a São Cristóvão, a roda habitual veria certamente um Machadinho mais gago, mais taciturno, mais suscetível" (*Machado* 105–106).

43. "lutava contra os impulsos dos nevropatas e os espevitamentos dos mestiços— dois perigos que o ameaçavam" (73).

44. "Um psicanalista talvez lhe descobrisse terríveis complexos, talvez, esmeril-hando-lhe os versos, neles vislumbrasse indícios reveladores, sobretudo na evocação da irmã, que se poderia ter tornado para ele o ideal feminino, tão pura e intensamente a amara na árida infância" (111).

45. "Gonçalves Dias viveu sempre a se vingar das mulheres—a vingar-se, nos corpos, do carinho, da compreensão que não lhes conseguia encontrar nas corações" (111).

46. "Esperava tranquilamente a sua hora, sem sombra de *mulatice* intelectual" (83).

47. "[e]ntre os brancos dominadores e os negros escravos ficaram os índios e os mestiços, que escolheram viver na indolência e no ociosidade" (134).

48. "A ela, ao sangue—ou aos sangues—que transmitiu ao poeta, emprestam todavia todos a maior importância, sendo unânimes todos quantos sobre Gonçalves Dias escreveram, desde Sílvio Romero e José Veríssimo até hoje, em proclamar que o seu temperamento se explica pela herança combinada das três raças—a portuguesa, do pai, a índia e a negra, da mãe" (*Gonçalves* 13).

49. Freyre continued to develop his theory that the Portuguese have a special ability to adapt to tropical regions and to learn the ways of their indigenous peoples. His version of the widespread belief in the Portuguese ability to "whiten" darker people has become known in English as Lusotropicalism. See Freyre's *O mundo que o Português criou*.

50. "[e]sse sentimento da inferioridade racial, de que só nos veio libertar Gilberto Freyre, a todos oprimia" (*Prosa* 241).

51. I consciously employ the masculine form "mestizo" because it reflects the gender bias inherent in these discussions.

52. It is often difficult for those outside a Brazilian frame of reference regarding race to understand how an individual could undergo whitening. See Carl Degler's *Neither Black nor White: Slavery and Race Relations in Brazil and the United States* for a comparative approach to the idea of race in those two countries.

53. "O livro possibilita a afirmação inequívoca de um povo que se debatia ainda com as ambigüidades de sua própria definição. Ele se transforma em unicidade nacional. Ao retrabalhar a problemática da cultura brasileira, Gilberto Freyre oferece ao brasileiro uma carteira de identidade. A ambigüidade da identidade do Ser nacional forjada pelos intelectuais do Século XIX não podia resistir mais tempo. Ela havia se tornado incompatível com o processo de desenvolvimento econômico e social do país . . .[N]os anos 30 procura-se transformar radicalmente o conceito de homem brasileiro. Qualidades como 'preguiça,' 'indolência,' consideradas como inerentes à raça mestiça, são substituídas por uma ideologia do trabalho." (42)

54. "deve ter sentido a diferença entre o *pardinho* que nascera havia quase setenta anos na casinhola do Livramento, e o *escritor* que morria cercado da consideração de todos . . ." (284).

55. "Realmente, Gonçalves Dias foi mais brasileiro, pela inspiração, pela sensibilidade e pela forma, do que todos os poetas que o precedera; o que não sabemos é se não o seria do mesmo modo se apenas fosse mulato, ou cafuzo, ou mesmo branco" (*Gonçalves* 135).

56. "O próprio temperamento e o meio em que viveu podê-lo-iam, por se sós, ter tornado permeável às nossas coisas. Poder-se-á objetar que esse temperamento foi fruto dos três sangues que lhe corriam nas veias. Não resta dúvida sobre isso. Mas como distinguir o que lhe veio do branco, ou do índio, ou do negro? Ao passo que não é difícil saber o que recebeu da sua época, e das condições de sua vida." (135)

57. "qualquer poeta que tivesse nascido com a Independência e começado a escrever quando mal se solidificava o Império, numa época de intenso nacionalismo" (135).

Chapter Three. From Consumption to Production: Victoria Ocampo as Cultural Critic

1. "Si se considera el conjunto de los trabajos publicados, la mayor parte se centra en V. Ocampo, principalmente en su personalidad literaria, y colateralmente—como parte de su obra—se menciona la revista" (68).

2. Recent exceptions to this trend include studies by Molloy and Masiello.

3. "En este sentido no difiere mayormente la actitud del autobiógrafo hombre de la autobiógrafa mujer y el cliché de cierta 'escritura feminina', hecha toda de interiores y ajena a la historia, se vuelve relativo: aplicable no a toda mujer que escribe sino a aquellas (la mayoría) cuya figuración pública es reducida, no asumida o no reconocida" (Molloy "Dos" 293).

4. "al no corresponder la autobiografía hispanoamericana con supuestos modelos del género (pongamos por caso, contextos autobiográficos europeos del siglo XIX), se la desdeña como híbrido, sin ver que esa misma hibridez es lo que la vuelve distintiva. Así la autobiografía hispanoamericana ha pasado a desempeñar una función ingrata: la de texto subalterno, fuente de datos para la historia literaria, apéndice de la obra de un escritor pero carente de valor propio" ("Dos" 279).

5. See, for example, Ocampo's prefaces to volumes 2 and 6 of the *Testimonios*.

6. "cuando me he propuesto describir a un personaje que nada tiene que ver con mi circunstancia, cuando he querido limitarme a un análisis *objetivo,* he caído pronto en la cuenta de que estaba refiriéndome a un ser jamás visto como si perteneciera a mi vida íntima." "¿existe otra vía para comprender a fondo a una persona? Si existe, yo no he transitado por ella. Cuando mis *Testimonios* alcanzan un nivel de *High Fidelity* es que por ese camino andan" (*Testimonios* 6 8).

7. "Mi única ambición es llegar a escribir un día, más o menos bien, más o menos mal, pero como una mujer. Si la imagen de Aladino poseyese una lámpara maravillosa, y por su mediación me fuera dado el escribir en el estilo de un Shakespeare, de un Dante, de un Goethe, de un Cervantes, de un Dostoiewsky, realmente no aprovecharía la ganga. Pues entiendo que una mujer no puede aliviarse de sus sentimientos y pensamientos en un estilo masculino, del mismo modo que no puede hablar con voz de hombre" (*Testimonios* 1 12).

8. "La consecuencia que saco de mis reflexiones sobre este tema es que nada de esto habría ocurrido si yo no hubiera sido americana. Si yo no hubiera sido esencialmente americana yo no habría hablado un español empobrecido, improprio para expresar todo matiz, y no me habría negado al español de ultramar. . . . Si no hubiese sido americana, en fin, no experimentaría tampoco, probablemente, esta sed de explicar, de explicarnos y de explicarme. En Europa, cuando una cosa se produce, diríase que está explicada de antemano. . . . Entonces, henos aquí obligados a cerrar los ojos y a avanzar penosamente, a tientas, hacia nosotros mismos; a buscar en qué sentido pueden acomodarse las viejas explicaciones a los nuevos problemas. Vacilamos, tropezamos, nos engañamos, temblamos, pero seguimos obstinados. Aunque los resultados obtenidos fueran, por el momento mediocres, ¿que importa?" (*Testimonios* 1 39–40).

9. "He dicho antes que yo no me tengo por escritora, que ignoro totalmente el oficio. Que soy un simple ser humano en busca de expresión" (*Testimonios* 1 41).

Pedro Henríquez Ureña highlights this "quest for expression" as a leit motif of Latin American writing in general. His Charles Eliot Norton Lectures on Latin American literature, delivered at Harvard University in 1940–1941, were announced under the title "In Search of Expression."

10. See, for example, Janet Greenberg's "A Question of Blood: the Conflict of Sex and Class in the *Autobiografía* of Victoria Ocampo."

11. Ocampo delivered the speech upon receiving the Society's Premio de Honor.

12. "lo que se consideraba conveniente enseñar a las mujeres de mi clase," "imagino que en las clases pobres la enseñanza debía ser nula," "la gramática (léase la ortografía), una aritmética elemental, mucho catecismo, historia sagrada, un poco de historia universal, otro poco de historia argentina, algunas vagas nociones de ciencias naturales, idiomas (especialmente francés o inglés) . . . el piano" (*Testimonios* 5 16).

13. "Mi punto de vista era el de una adolescente capaz, cuyas dotes no puede aprovechar ni desarrollar plenamente por vía de un educación adecuada, *y que lo intuye a diario*" (16).

14. "El descubrimiento del *De Profundis* de Wilde bajo mi almohada alcanzó las proporciones de una catástrofe. El tomo fue confiscado por la censura casera sin que yo comprendiera el motivo, lo que aumentó mi indignación. Yo tenía, entonces, mis diecinueve años requetecumplidos" (*Testimonios* 5 18).

15. "Y no podía escapar a este proceso, puesto que deseaba principalmente dirigirme a mis compatriotas" (*Testimonios* 5 20).

16. See *Testimonios* 1 23.

17. "La lengua extranjera, en las mujeres del origen de Victoria Ocampo, era utilizada para escribir cartas, leer novelitas, recitar un poco o asistir a representaciones teatrales, hablar con los tenderos o los modistas, ir a la peluquería. La lengua extranjera era lengua de consumo femenino y no de producción.

"Victoria Ocampo la subvierte, volviéndola lengua productiva: leer, recibir, pero también citar, devolver. Los idiomas extranjeros no son sólo medios del consumo material o simbólico sino que, en el caso de Victoria Ocampo, son medios de producción" (*Modernidad* 91).

18. Through *Sur,* Ocampo commissioned many translations, including works by Aldous Huxley, D. H. Lawrence, Carl Jung, André Malraux, Virginia Woolf, Graham Greene, Thomas Mann, H. G. Wells, William Faulkner, T. E. Lawrence, Jean-Paul Sartre, Albert Camus, and Katherine Anne Porter. See *Testimonios* 10 for the extensive list of works translated by Ocampo herself.

19. "Lo que su medio social pensaba como adorno, Victoria Ocampo lo convierte en instrumento" (*Modernidad* 91). In her latest book, *La máquina cultural: maestras, traductores y vanguardistas* (1998), Sarlo takes a less positive view of Ocampo's activities in the chapter she dedicates to her. Though Sarlo makes brief reference to the importance of the cultural space she opened, Ocampo is criticized for not having taken enough risks (130). Whereas her earlier writings place Ocampo in an active role, Sarlo now suggests she is a translating machine with little self-control. See Aira, who describes Ocampo as lacking both talent and intelligence (65), for a more extreme version of this type of critique.

20. "Estas dos palabras no se dirigen, ni a los dantólogos, ni a los letrados, pues

nada puedo yo enseñarles. Dirígense a los simples lectores, a aquellos que podrían amar este grande y hermoso libro y que, por una u otra razón, aún no se acercaron a él. Dirígense, sobre todo, a quienes lo han hojeado perezosamente" (*De Francesca* 18).

21. "Cuando nos acercamos a Dante, sea cual fuere el camino seguido, tropiézase uno bruscamente con una guardia numerosa y terrible: los comentaristas" (7).

22. "Erizados de erudición, yérguense en agresiva actitud sobre el umbral de cada canto del Poema; y sus interpretaciones—que con frecuencia se contradicen unas a otras—blandidas como alabardas, hacen retrodecer al lector medroso *là dove il sol tace*" (7).

23. Ocampo discusses how Angel de Estrada read her book this way in her *Autobiografía 3*, 106.

24. "no debe escribirse sobre la *Divina Comedia* si uno no trae un dato o una interpretación nuevos. Aparentemente, no es su caso. Usted sabe el francés, pero no es su idioma. ¿Por qué no escribe en español? (Curioso consejo viniendo de quien venía. '¿Y usted?,' hubiese podido replicarle.) ¿Por qué, además, no elige otro género de tema menos dantesco, por no decir pedantesco, si es que siente verdadera necesidad de escribir? Por ejemplo, experiencias personales, directamente vividas, etc." (*Testimonios 5* 22).

25. "Victoria Ocampo es una escritora por naturaleza . . . Y qué encantadora postura de humildad la suya. Con qué gesto tan femenino abre la puerta segura de la eterna desesperanza" (qtd. in Muschietti 82).

26. "Es usted, Señora, una ejemplar aparición de feminidad" (128).

27. "El fuerte de la mujer no es saber sino sentir. Saber las cosas es tener sus conceptos y definiciones, y esto es obra de varón" (158).

28. "Debo confesarle que he leído a Dante con amor, simplemente, y que lo he leído de una manera activa, no pasiva" (*Testimonios 1* 190).

29. "tal vez no haya habido, en todas la literaturas modernas, otra mujer dotada de parejo ímpetu poético" (*Testimonios 1* 316).

30. "El no nos disimula que, en su concepción de la mujer, el genio lírico no ocupa lugar alguno. Cree que la mujer es un género, no un individuo, y con toda cortesía lo subraya" (*Testimonios 1* 316).

31. "Si Ortega estima que sólo el género epistolar se aviene a la feminidad, es—y así lo proclama—porque la carta se dirige a un solo ser, no a todos, y porque, al revés del hombre, la mujer está hecho [sic] para la intimidad" (319).

32. "¿supone acaso Ortega que las cartas de Marie de Rabutin-Chantal sobre el casamiento de Mademoiselle o la muerte de Turena fueron redactadas con menos atención al público que los poemas de Anna de Noailles o las novelas de Virginia Woolf?" (321).

33. "Según Ortega, el hombre y la mujer no pueden alcanzar su máxima expansión sino en dos atmósferas distintas. Para el hombre, la vida pública; para la mujer, la vida privada" (319).

34. "[C]reo que los escritores de raza, cualquiera que sea su sexo o su modo de expresión, escriben ante todo para sí mismos, para librarse de sí mismos, para llegar a una clarificación de sí mismos, para comunicarse consigo mismos. Pues sólo comunica con los demás quien ha comunicado antes consigo mismo. Y ¿qué es eso del *público* de que habla Ortega? Unas cuantas personas, no más" (321).

35. In her recounting of the debate between Ocampo and Ortega y Gasset, Greenberg criticizes Ocampo for agreeing with his implied hierarchy of the genres (her style of writing being inferior to fiction or poetry) while arguing against his views on women's roles. Greenberg argues that Ocampo's position reveals "identity problems" that underlie the *Testimonios* ("Divided" 56). I disagree. As Greenberg herself notes, Ortega y Gasset was a powerful person in the field who could (and did) help Ocampo launch her career.

36. "[N]o se le ocurre al autor oferecerse como fuente histórica. Sólo aspira a que sus recuerdos dispersos sean leídos con el agrado con que puede leerse una coleción de historietas y retratos del natural y las consiguientes reflexiones marginales" (*Visto* 9).

37. Sylvia Molloy notes as much in her review of King's book (108).

38. "En el dominio literario *Sur* puso, por encima de todo, la calidad del escritor, cualesquiera fuesen sus tendencias. Las letras no tienen nada que ver con el sufragio universal, ni con la democracia, ni con la caridad cristiana: o se vale o no se vale" (Ocampo *Sur* 303–305, Nov. 1966–Apr. 1967: 16).

39. "Precisamente porque soy una americana auténtica no siento la necesidad de escupir al rostro de ningún español destrozado . . . como tampoco siento la necesidad de matar al que no opina como yo para convencerle de que estoy en lo cierto. Querría Dios que sea siempre ésta la auténtica americanidad y que el destino no nos lleve, algún día, al callejón sin salida de la violencia" (32: 71).

40. "Las guerras o revoluciones, las mantanzas, en una palabra, me horrorizan y nunca admitiré que sean una manera de resolver problemas de ningún orden, quizá porque nosotras las mujeres estamos acostumbradas en tiempos de paz y de guerra a arriesgar nuestra vida; pero para dar vida y no muerte" (32: 71).

41. "¿se le ha ocurrido a usted jamás el pensar que ha existido y existe aún en el mundo otra explotación más odiosa que ésta: la de la mujer por el hombre? Me refiero a la posición de inferioridad absoluta en que se han visto obligadas a vivir, desde hace siglos, las mujeres, y que comienza hoy a variar. Me refiero a las condiciones de *existencia no privilegiada* a las que el hombre las ha reducido por la fuerza en todas las clases sociales. Me refiero a la humillación de haber sido tratadas por las leyes de los hombres, durante siglos, como menores de edad, como incapaces, como insanas a quienes se les niega responsabilidad verdadera" (32: 73).

42. "Ese 'ciertas', a quien naturalmente le crecen las comillas, ya sabemos lo que significa. Y bien; esas alusiones, esas comillas latentes, esa aparición del sexo en el momento en que quiere usted hacerme sentir su menosprecio son indignos de usted, José Bergamín" (32: 73).

43. "'Como la que la lleva a Ud., a esa desdichada comparación feminista entre sus delicados sufrimientos de mujer secreta (sin entre comillas) y los del proletariado trabajador. ¡Que Dios le perdone, Victoria Ocampo, esa . . . delicada coquetería!'" In his recounting of the debate, King characterizes Bergamín's remarks as "masterly," agreeing with him that Ocampo's position reveals "'delicada coquetería'" (33: 104).

44. "en cuanto a mi desdichada comparación feminista, acabo de encontrarla bajo la pluma de E. Mounier . . . Bergamín no ha de tener, para desconfiar de este *señor*, las mismas razones que parece tener para desconfiar de mí" (33: 104).

45. "La imposibilidad, para la persona, de nacer a su vida propia,—que a nuestro parecer define el proletariado todavía más esencialmente que la miseria material,—es

el destino de casi todas las mujeres, ricas y pobres, burguesas, obreras y campesinas" (qtd. in *Sur* 33: 105).

46. "La lógica es atributo del hombre . . . , la intuición de la mujer. El hombre es un ser racional, la mujer es un ser irracional. El hombre tiende al mundo de lo abstracto, de las ideas puras, al panlogismo. La mujer se mueve mejor en el mundo de lo concreto, de la ideas impuras, de lo ilógico" (32).

47. "las creaciones del hombre más vinculadas a su inconciencia, como la poesía o el arte, serían la expresión de su feminidad. Y, en rigor, ¿qué más femenino que el arte, aunque (*o porque*) sea realizado por hombres" (34).

48. "La sociedad moderna virilizó a la mujer, falsificando, con graves consecuencias psíquicas, la esencia de su ser. . . . Si es que la radical crisis de nuestro tiempo ha de ser superada, habrá que volver a una mujer femenina" (45).

49. "el sexo, que para la mujer es básico, casi no tiene importancia en el acto propiamente sexual" (Sábato 209–210: 35).

50. "La virtud de la mujer se centra en su altruísmo por la especie, en su capacidad de sacrificio personal en honor a los hijos y a los hombres bajo su cuidado. Por eso su mundo es concreto y pequeño, personal y vital. Pero de ahí a las pequeñeces y, lo que es peor, a la pequeñez hay un paso. Y al egoísmo de hormiga, al comadreo, al chismorreo pequeño, a los celos viscerales. El hombre también se equivoca, pero al menos se equivoca haciendo una guerra mundial o un sistema filosófico" (Sábato 209–210: 36).

51. "En un modestísimo y casi invisible parágrafo puse una microscópica lista de defectos y ya usted se me viene encima como una furiosa bacante, dispuesta a desgarrarme vivo y a comerme crudo. Cálmese, Victoria. No es para tanto" (213–214: 159). Sábato refers here to the paragraph quoted above.

52. "Su carta requiere algunas urgentes aclaraciones, pues siendo mi trabajo más largo, menos pintoresco y epistolar, más abstracto, menos femenino en fin que su somero dictamen, corro el riesgo que muchos prefieran conocer mis ideas por las suyas" (213–214: 158).

53. "En cuanto a las opiniones de Malraux sobre las mujeres, me aduce usted que una vez, conversando con él, etc. Las reuniones íntimas, los tés, las comidas, las conversaciones tienen algún valor para juzgar la personalidad de un escritor. Pero lo más auténtico de un novelista, lo más profunda y misteriosamente suyo, no lo va a oír de sus labios sino de los labios de sus personajes, a veces de los menos sospechosos" (159–160).

54. "He respondido a su largo y meritorio ensayo de divulgación con una cartita de morondanga. Pero así como un ensayo no tiene la obligación de adoptar el estilo epistolar, una carta no tiene la obligación de parecerse a un ensayo" (162).

55. "Me gustan las enumeraciones. Tiene un airecito ordenado, sea cual fuere el desbarajuste de la mercadería que cubren" (162).

56. See especially Janet Greenberg's "The Divided Self" (unpublished dissertation), which is the only study to focus extensively on the *Testimonios*.

57. Translated by David Garnett. See also the prefaces to Ocampo's *Testimonios,* particularly volumes 4 and 6, for further references to subjective criticism.

58. "Desde el momento en que escribimos, estamos condenados a no poder hablar más que de nosotros, de lo que hemos visto con nuestros ojos, sentido con nuestra sensibilidad, comprendido con nuestra inteligencia. Imposible escapar a esta ley" (*Testimonios* 1 26).

59. "En esta América en que todo está 'in the making', los testimonios son quizá más necesarios que en ninguna otra parte, y si los míos significan algo es sobre todo porque pertenezco a ella" (*Testimonios* 2 8).

60. We might recall that Greenberg is applying to Ocampo's work a theory developed to analyze women's writing outside Latin America in the nineteenth century.

61. "[L]os artículos de esta nueva serie y las conferencias... no están solamente en mis cajones: están en diarios, en revistas y en manos de algunos amigos. No es totalmente improbable que se le ocurra a alguien, el día de mi ausencia definitiva, recoger estas páginas dispersas. Prefiero adelantarme y publicarlas yo misma, por insuficientes que me parezcan. Además, no queda descartado que éstos como otros testimonios puedan servir a su hora, como puntos de referencia" (7).

62. Ocampo published Borges's translation of *A Room of One's Own* through the Editorial Sur in 1937. Excerpts of this and other translations of Woolf's work also appeared in *Sur*.

63. "Cuando, sentada junto a su chimenea, Virginia, me alejaba de la niebla y de la soledad; cuando tendía mis manos hacia el calor y tendía entre nosotras un puente de palabras... ¡qué rica era, no obstante! No de su riqueza, pues esa llave que supo usted encontrar, y sin la cual jamás entramos en posesión de nuestro propio tesoro (aunque lo llevemos, durante toda nuestra vida, colgado al cuello), de nada puede servirme si no la encuentro por mí misma. Rica de mi probreza, esto es: de mi hambre" (*Testimonios* 1 10).

64. "son una serie de testimonios de mi hambre. ¡De mi hambre, tan auténticamente americana!" (*Testimonios* 1 11).

65. *Testimonios* 1 12. The quotation appears in English with "south" and "american" in lowercase.

66. "Y si, como usted espera, Virginia, todo esfuerzo, por oscuro que sea, es convergente y apresura el nacimiento de una forma de expresión que todavía no ha encontrado una temperatura propicia a su necesidad de florecer, vaya mi esfuerzo a sumarse al de tantas mujeres, desconocidas o célebres, como en el mundo han trabajado" (*Testimonios* 1 17).

67. European authors and artists are the primary focus of roughly sixty percent of her writings while Latin American and U.S. authors and artists are each the focus of approximately twenty percent of Ocampo's essays.

68. "Gabriela: las 'aubépines' respiradas por Proust y que lo inundaban de una felicidad sin nombre, de la cual no sabía qué hacerse, son vecinos de tus almendros. No hay un espacio tan grande, créeme, entre Combray y tu Valle de Elqui. Mi corazón ha medido la distancia" (181).

69. The essays were published as *Emily Brontë (Terra Incognita)* (Buenos Aires: Sur, 1938) and *Virginia Woolf, Orlando & Cía.* (Buenos Aires: Sur, 1938).

70. "Voy a hablarles a ustedes como 'common reader' de la obra de Virginia Woolf. Voy a hablarles de la imagen que conservo de ella. No esperen ustedes oír crítica literaria pura; se decepcionarían" (*Testimonios* 2 13).

71. (Ocampo *Testimonios* 2 17–18). Ocampo does not include bibliographical information for her citations here. In this case, Ocampo translated the quotation, which is from *The Common Reader,* page 150, into Spanish.

72. Borges worked on *Proa,* and he and the remaining three worked on *Martín Fierro.* Among the lists of names of the founders of and contributors to these magazines, the only woman who appears is Norah Lange, who was one of the editors of *Martín Fierro.* This and other information about the magazines appears in María Luisa Bastos's *Borges ante la crítica literaria argentina: 1923–1960* (17–150).

73. "Hoy, preguntar: ¿es usted de Boedo o de Florida?—es como decir—: ¿Es usted un hombre o es un tilingo?" (qtd. in Bastos 52).

74. "[l]a historia del pasado contenido en el presente hasta desbordarlo; es la historia de su turbadora simultaneidad. Es también la historia de los lazos invisibles que ligan a los seres humanos unos a otros" (19).

75. "Y como la vida sin más difiere de la vida en literatura así como el verde en la naturaleza difiere del verde en un poema, la existencia de Orlando oscila perpetuamente entre estos dos polos, desde el final del siglo XVI hasta nuestros días . . ." (30).

76. "El descubrimiento de un espíritu a través de un libro se vuelve un acontecimiento de tal magnitud en este ser, que lo deja como anonadado de felicidad durante días enteros, ciego y sordo a todo lo demás" (3).

77. See Sylvia Molloy's "The theatrics of reading: body and book in Victoria Ocampo" in *At Face Value* for a discussion of the powerful exchange between the "read" and the "lived" in Ocampo's life and writings.

78. "que los artistas ponen su perfección en sus obras y no en su vida, fuera de sí mismos y no en sí mismos" (43).

79. She recounts such a misunderstanding with Hermann von Keyserling in her book *El viajero y una de sus sombras* (Buenos Aires: Sudamericana, 1951).

80. "Orlando no *representa* su pasión de la literatura, su sentimiento del tiempo y su rebeldía ante la situación de inferioridad impuesta a la mujer: Orlando las vive" (54).

81. "Orlando hembra se daba cuenta de que las mujeres no son naturalmente ni obedientes, ni castas, ni perfumadas, ni revestidas de adornos, y que sólo llegan a serlo sometiéndose a la más molesta disciplina" (39).

82. "A cada página nos entran deseos de comentar a la comentadora a través de su comentario" (*Testimonios* 2 59).

83. "por entonces Virginia Woolf apenas había publicado su primera novela, mientras que yo soñaba con la letra de molde como con un imposible" (*Testimonios* 2 55–56).

84. Marinetti was present when Ocampo gave a speech at the P.E.N. Club in Buenos Aires in which she referred to herself as a common reader (*Testimonios* 2 58).

85. "La manera de leer que usted ejercita (lo que yo iba a llamar en 1936, manera del 'common reader') no es injusta e indebida . . . Es, en efecto, la única manera de leer que existe, y el resto es erudición. La lectura, en su más noble forma, constituye un lujo espiritual, no es estudio, aprendizaje, adquisición de noticias útiles para la lucha social. Es un virtual aumento y dilatación que ofrecemos a nuestras germinaciones

interiores; merced a ella conseguimos realizar lo que sólo como posibilidad latía en nosotros." (qtd. in *Testimonios* 2 57)

86. A este título y bajo este título es como Virginia Woolf nos habla de Montaigne, Defoe, Jane Austen, George Eliot, Addison, Conrad, Meredith, Hardy, Swift, las Brontë, etc., y puedo agregarles que es imposible descubrir, en el caso de ella, rastro de ignorancia.

Hablar en nombre del "common reader" era, pues, una elección mucho menos modesta que lo que pudiera parecer a primera vista. Si todos los "common readers" fueran de la talla de Virginia, los grandes escritores no tendrían por qué quejarse de su público. (58)

87. See, for example, King's *Sur*.

88. "[e]l problema de la mujer en cuanto escritora, está tratado en esas páginas con una fuerza y una sutileza extraordinarias" (71).

89. "un crítico de izquierda (¿y no es una desdicha que los críticos dejen transparentar sus pasiones políticas cuando hablan de literatura?) reprochaba hace poco a Virginia Woolf el que sólo describiera, como Proust, los sofrimientos de la flor y nata de la burguesía parasitaria" (71).

90. "resulta difícil adorar devotamente a Napoleón, no encontrarle defectos, y creer al mismo tiempo en la emancipación de la mujer. Quisiera agregar que esto vale también para Mussolini y para Hitler" (73).

91. "el encanto del rostro de Virginia Woolf . . . encanto del más feliz encuentro de lo material y lo espiritual en una cara de mujer" (77).

92. "fea o desprovista de encanto femenino; que toda mujer preocupada por defender los derechos de la mujer debe ser repulsiva, desdichada en el matrimonio o solterona chiflada" (84).

93. "La prosa que Virginia habita es así . . . Las sillas, las mesas, las paredes, la flor, el libro, el caracol, el Picasso que pasan por sus manos nos hablan de ella antes y por encima de todo. ¿Por qué ha elegido este caracol, y no aquel otro? . . . ¿Qué es lo que va a preferir? ¿Qué va a subrayar? ¿A quién se va a acercar más? ¿Qué nos dice a propósito de la novela moderna?" (60)

94. "Si algún ser humano ha habido que se confundiera con el lugar que lo vió nacer y con los objetos que los rodearon, fué sin duda Emily Brontë" (97).

95. "Este libro es un lugar, a imagen del título que lleva. Pero este lugar, señalado en los mapas de Inglaterrra, es más que Inglaterra: es el alma de Emily Brontë. El alma de Emily Brontë, aquí, en América, y en cualquier región del mundo tanto como en Inglaterra" (97).

96. "Así los más enraizados en su tierra la mezclan a todas las tierras. Y quizá nunca haya comprendido yo mejor lo que significaba para mí el grande y áspero viento de las pampas con su carga de teros gritones que al escuchar gemir el de *Wuthering Heights*" (98).

97. "Cada ser lleva dentro de sí la misma escena, el mismo drama desde que nace a la conciencia y por todo el resto de su vida; y representa su escena, su drama, cualesquiera que sean los acontecimientos o los personajes que le salgan al paso hasta dar con su acontecimiento, su personaje. Tal vez no los encuentre nunca. Pero eso no le impide representar su escena, su drama, y dar los acontecimientos y a los personajes

que menos se prestan a entrar en su juego la forma del acontecimiento y del personaje que son los suyos. Pues ha venido al mundo para una sola escena, un solo drama, y no puede menos de repetirlos a lo largo de toda su existencia" (*Testimonios* 2 115).

98. "La manera más directa de entrar en contacto con ella (además de sus escritos) es hacer el inventario de cuanto la rodeaba" (99).

99. "su amor a lo que tiene límite y puede por consiguiente ser nombrado; su amor a lo que no tiene límite y, por consiguiente, no puede aprisionarse en palabras, no puede ser nombrado" (153–154).

100. "Cuando Heathcliff dice a Nelly: 'Mi espíritu está tan eternamente recluído, vuelto hacia dentro, que estoy a veces tentado de volverlo hacia afuera, hacia alguien', es Emily la que nos está contando cómo y por qué ha sido escrito *Wuthering Heights*" (154).

101. "Los grandes artistas producen, a mi entender, dos especies de obras, de acuerdo con su naturaleza, con las circunstancias de su vida: unas son compensatorias, las otras complementarias" (155).

102. "Anna de Noailles el poeta que escribía y la mujer con quien uno se encontraba parecían dos seres diferentes" (156).

103. "Se siente que en la vida gusta con fruición lo que sigue gustando en sus libros. Pasamos de la mujer a la obra, de la obra a la mujer, sin dar tumbos" (156).

104. "sólo se atrevía a vivir de acuerdo con su temperamento por medio de ellos. Su pasión, su violencia, su tumulto estalla en ellos, rompe en ellos todos los diques con fuerza tanto más terrible cuanto que no encuentra otra salida" (157).

105. "Porque Heathcliff era un niño huraño y de piel morena las malas lenguas decían de él: 'An american or spanish castaway'—un americano o español abandonado. Aquí Heathcliff está, pues, en su casa. Aquí, es América y todavía España" (164–165).

106. "Quiero pedirle aquí perdón, pues mi amor a ella es exacto. Exacto como todo lo que es amor y no curiosidad" (163).

107. "la crónica de una mujer que en un país de machos condescendientes se atrevió a pensar y a sentir y amar como se le dió la gana" (47).

Chapter Four. Nation and Motherhood in Gabriela Mistral

1. "decía que el espectáculo más maravilloso que puede darse—espectáculo superior al de una perfecta obra de arte—consiste en la visión de una bella criatura humana 'que además tenga un cerebro'" (*Testimonios* 1 55).

2. "cuando se observa aquel rostro de una rara belleza material y espiritual, es imposible evitar el pensamiento de que nadie mejor que Ruskin debió merecer esta frase por él dedicada a otros: 'Una cosa espléndida a la cual mirar, una cosa admirable a la cual hablar'" (55).

3. Any "hablar," as she terms it, between Ruskin and Ocampo would perforce be readerly, as Ruskin died in 1900.

4. "¿Cómo puede ignorar que hay ocasiones en que el lector grita con razón: '¡Qué bien está esto! ¡Es exactamente lo que pienso!', sin tener por ello la sabiduría del autor cuyo libro lee?" (61).

5. "All the higher circles of human intelligence are, to those beneath, only momentarily and partially open" (Ruskin 12).

6. Mistral includes an unidentified fragment of the speech which she retitles "Misión de la mujer." It appears on page 99 of Wiley's 1889 edition of *Sesame and Lilies.*

7. "Mujer-madre-maternidad se han hecho sinónimos del mensaje poético mistralino como resultado de la valoración patriarcal y paternalista de su persona y producción poética" (47).

8. Similarly, in "Women, Literature, and National Brotherhood," Mary Louise Pratt proposes a rereading of Mistral's posthumously published *Poema de Chile,* a collection largely ignored by literary critics. She suggests that the marginalization of this work is due to nationalist, public overtones: it does not conform to the established view of Mistral that confines her to the domestic and the personal.

9. "imitarían la acción de los misioneros católicos de la colonia, entre los indios que todavía no conocen el idioma castellano" (1226).

10. "¿Y por dónde ha de comenzar él que quiere hacer leer?"; "¿Hay en el mundo persona ilustrada que niegue que el comienzo de toda lectura culta está en los autores clásicos de la Humanidad?" (1252).

To cut costs, Vasconcelos established a press at the Ministry of Education. "Y con sorpresa aparecieron por toda la república los primeros ejemplares, en pasta verde, de Homero, Esquilo, Eurípides, Platón, Dante, Goethe, etc.; no llegué, ni con mucho, a los cien clásicos, sino apenas a diecisiete ediciones de más de veinticinco mil volúmenes la mayor parte de ellas" (1253).

11. "Cuando Sarmiento consumó su obra educativa en la Argentina, primero se aprendió de memoria a Horacio Mann; en seguida, por si algo se le olvidaba, acarreó con doscientas o trescientas maestras norteamericanas y las estableció en la pampa . . . Pero el caso de México no era el mismo. México tuvo Universidad antes que Boston, y bibliotecas, museos, diarios y teatro, antes que Nueva York y Philadelphia. En México basta con rascar un poco el subsuelo para que aparezcan los brotes de la vieja cultura enterrada por la barbarie de los gobiernos" (1263–1264).

12. "Todo lo que sé, poco, pero muy fértil en mi vida, ella, Europa, me lo ha dado" (qtd. in Jiménez 44).

13. "En la Capital, la Secretaría de Educación editaba los clásicos griegos, Plotino, los Evangelios y la Divina Comedia y en el Anfiteatro de la Preparatoria, decorado por Diego Rivera, y lleno de bote en bote, oímos la Sinfonías de Beethoven. Ahora había que rehacer, y sembrar, que instaurar el orden de la justicia y de la cultura y, como los campesinos van al campo con sus sacos de semillas, así nos enviaba Vasconcelos a todas partes—a cada quien a hacer lo que sabía, o a ensayarse en lo que soñaba, o a aprender, que, al cabo, todo era necesario para el pueblo hambriento de pan y de cultura" (v).

14. See chapter three of *Drawing the Line,* for an interesting discussion of the way in which the direct influence of these painters on the "New American Painters" such as Jackson Pollock was dismissed with the onset of the Cold War period.

15. Later in his life, Vasconcelos disavowed any connection with the muralists and other leftist revolutionaries.

16. Meyer and Sherman report that one landholder, Luiz Terrazas, still owned as much land as the total distributed by the administration. "It was true that he had multiplied by nine times the amount distributed by Carranza, but in 1924, seven years after the adoption of the Constitution, Article 27 had not yet benefitted the overwhelming majority of rural Mexicans" (576).

17. Ironically, the United States government refused to recognize his government for fear that it would lead to "bolshevikism." Obregón's response was to negotiate the 1923 Treaty of Bucareli which, voiding an article of Mexico's 1917 constitution, permitted U.S. oil companies to retain their Mexican holdings in exchange for diplomatic recognition.

18. *Excelsior*, 7–11 Apr. 1930, qtd. in O'Malley (58).

19. *El Popular*, 20 Feb. 1939, qtd. in O'Malley (134).

20. Baltasar Dromundo, "La Soldadera," in *Domingos Culturales*, circular no. 5: 53–54. Partido Nacional Revolucionario, 8 July 1930, qtd. in and trans. by O'Malley (134–135).

21. "Comprendí que un texto corresponde hacerlo a los maestros nacionales y no a una extranjera, y he recopilado esta obra sólo para la escuela mexicana que lleva mi nombre" (xiv).

22. "Mi pequeño trabajo no pretende competir con los textos nacionales, por cierto: tiene los defectos lógicos de la labor hecha por un viajero. . . . Un libro de esta índole es, a mi juicio, labor de tres años, y necesita mucha tranquilidad de espíritu y un profundo conocimiento del ambiente. Es éste el ensayo de un trabajo que realizaré algún día, en mi país, destinado a las mujeres de América. Las siento mi familia espiritual; escribo por ellas, tal vez sin preparación, pero con mucho amor" (xiii).

23. See Horan for a discussion of Mistral's acceptance of her place as "trick of the weak" ("Matrilineage" 456). Horan borrows the phrase from Josefina Ludmer's "Tretas del débil," in which Ludmer lays out Sor Juana's strategies for writing from a position of subordination and marginality.

24. The first collection, *Recados: Contando a Chile*, was anthologized by Alfonso M. Escudero in the year of her death, 1957. As examples of other anthologies, see the collections published by Roque Esteban Scarpa.

25. René Letona in "La prosa de Gabriela Mistral" notes of these articles: "Muchas tenían esa condición efímera propia del periodismo" (86). For other characerizations of her prose work, see M. Alejandra Ochoa P. "Poética explícita de los escritos en prosa de Gabriela Mistral," Gastón Figueira "Páginas desconocidas u olvidadas de Gabriela Mistral," Marta Baralis "Necesidad de estudiar y valorar la prosa de Gabriela Mistral," and Mire-Lise Gazarian-Gautier "La prosa de Gabriela Mistral, o una verdadera joya desconocida."

26. "Y sea profesionista, obrera, campesina o simple dama, su única razón de ser sobre el mundo es la maternidad, la material y la espiritual juntas, o la última en las mujeres que no tenemos hijos" (xiii).

27. For a discussion of Mistral's acceptance of her place in that order as a deliberate "trick of the weak," see Horan ("Matrilineage" 456).

28. "Tal vez en parte no pequeña hayan contribuido los *Libros de Lectura* sin índole

femenina, a esa especie de empañamiento del espíritu de familia que se va observando en las nuevas generaciones" (xiv).

29. "La participación, cada día más intensa, de las mujeres en las profesiones liberales y en las industriales trae una ventaja: su independencia económica, un bien indiscutible; pero trae también cierto desasimiento del hogar, y, sobre todo, una pérdida lenta del sentido de la maternidad" (xiv).

30. The version appearing in the *Lecturas* has been shortened. The citation below is from a longer version printed in a posthumous collection of Mistral's writings on Mexico titled *Croquis Mexicanos* (23–26).

31. "Madre mexicana: para buscar tus grandes modelos no volverás tus ojos hacia las mujeres locas del siglo, que danzan y se agitan en plazas y salones y apenas conocen al hijo que llevaron clavado en sus entrañas, las mezquinas mujeres que traicionan la vida al esquivar el deber, sin haber esquivado el goce. Tú volverás los ojos hacia los modelos antiguos y eternos: a las madres hebreas y a las madres romanas" (24).

32. "[T]ú no has de renunciar a las mil noches de angustia junto a tu niño con fiebre, ni has de permitir que la boca de tu hijo beba la leche de un pecho mercenario. Tú, amamantarás, tú mecerás, tú irás cargando el tirso de jazmines que la vida dejó caído sobre tu pecho" (23–24).

33. Sierra qtd. in Vaughan 203–204.

34. Jean Franco also remarks on the conventionality of Mistral's views on women's roles in *Plotting Women* (103).

35. Oh, Creador; bajo tu luz cantamos
porque otra vez nos vuelves la esperanza.
Como los surcos de la tierra alzamos
la exhalación de nuestras alabanzas.

Gracias a Ti por el glorioso día
en el que van a erguirse las acciones;
por la alborada llena de alegría
que baja al valle y a los corazones.

Se alcen las manos, las que tú tejiste,
frescas y vivas sobre las faenas.
Se alcen los brazos, que con luz heriste,
en un temblor ardiente de colmenas.

Somos planteles de hijas todavía;
haznos el alma recta y poderosa
para ser dignas en el sumo día
en que seremos el plantel de esposas.

Venos crear a tu honda semejanza
con voluntad insigne de hermosura;
trenzar, trenzar divinas de confianza,
el lino blanco con la lana pura.

Mira cortar el pan de las espigas;
poner los frutos en la clara mesa;
tejer la juncia que nos es amiga:

¡crear, crear mirando a tu belleza!
Oh, Creador de manos soberanas,
sube el fruto en la canción ansiosa,
que ahora somos el plantel de hermanas,
pero seremos el plantel de esposas. (112–113)

36. English translation by David Ossman and Carlos B. Hagen in *Pablo Neruda: The Early Poems* (29). Mistral omitted the third and fourth stanzas:

"Maestranzas de la noche"

Fierro negro que duerme, fierro negro que gime
por cada poro un grito de desconsolación.
Las cenizas ardidas sobre la tierra triste . . .
Los caldos en que el bronce derritió su dolor . . .

Cada máquina tiene una pupila abierta
para mirarme a mí.

En las paredes cuelgan las interrogaciones,
florece en la bigornias el alma de los bronces,
y hay un temblor de pasos en los cuartos desiertos.

Y entre la noche negra, desesperadas, corren
y sollozan las almas de los obreros muertos . . . (*Lecturas* 111)

37. "[i]ngenua y feliz como los niños y como los pueblos que no tienen historia . . . Desnuda de política, de prensa, de guerras, de industrias y de negocios es la larga vacación de los hombres y el reinado sin crónica ni cronistas de las mujeres" (*Obra* 490).

38. See Elizabeth Garrels's "Piedra Azul, or the Colonial Paradise of Women" for a discussion of de la Parra's willful exclusion of history, which Garrels considers "perverse . . . in a time of such historical intensity" in Venezuela (138).

39. It is worth noting, as Ana Pizarro does, that though Mistral was born in rural Chile, she spent much of her life living and working in large urban centers (44).

40. "Pide para él la escuela soleada y limpia; pide los alegres parques; pide las fiestas de las imágenes, en el libro y en el cinema educador; exige colaborar en las leyes, pero cuando se trate de las cosas que te manchan o te empequeñecen la vida, puedes pedir leyes que limpien de vergüenza al hijo ilegítimo al que se hace nacer paria y vivir paria en medio de los otros hijos, y leyes que relgamentan vuestro trabajo y el de los niños, que se agotan en la faena brutal de las fábricas" (*Lecturas* 91).

41. See chapter three, "Feminism and Social Motherhood, 1890–1938," in Miller's *Latin American Women and the Search for Social Justice* for a discussion of Latin American feminism and motherhood in this period.

42. "Nuestra raza se probará en tus hijos; en ellos hemos de salvarnos o de perecer. Dios les fijó la dura suerte de que la marejada del Norte rompa sobre su pecho. Por eso, cuando tus hijos luchan o cantan, los rostros del Sur se vuelven hacia acá, llenos de esperanza y de inquietud a la par" (91).

43. "tu vientre sustenta a la raza; las muchedumbres ciudadanas nacen de tu seno calladamente"; "[h]ermosa y fuerte la tierra en que te tocó nacer, madre mexicana: tiene los frutos más perfectos del mundo y cuaja el algodón de copo más suave y

deleitoso"; "Tú eres *la colaboradora de la tierra* y por eso ella te baña de gracia en la luz de cada mañana" (90–91).

44. See Guillén de Nicolau's "Introducción" and Molloy's "Introduction."

45. "A menudo [Mistral] daba versiones equívocas, perfectamente capaz de dejar correr por la superficie una historia que sugería pistas falsas. A veces la coartada se convertía en verdad, repetida generación tras generación . . . Al escribir "Los sonetos de la muerte" ella misma genera la ficción coloreada por la tragédia. Convierte un episodio marginal en la chispa que hace cundir el incendio dentro del bosque. Crea literariamente un mito que se expande y exalta la imaginación de los lectores" (26).

46. He quotes Mistral on the subject: "Esos versos fueron escritos sobre una historia real. Pero Romelio Ureta no se suicidó por mí. Todo aquello ha sido novelería" (qtd. in Teitelboim 26).

47. "¿Cúal era ese 'amor imposible'? ¿Existía? . . . Existía. Exisitía el príncipe azul de la Cenicienta. Era rico, hermoso" (27).

Teitelboim's evidence is a letter from Mistral to Matilde Ladrón de Guevara: "'Usted, que comprende todo, tiene que haber comprendido también que ese amor no es precisamente el amor que inspiró 'Los sonetos de la muerte'. ¡Fue un segundo amor, hermana!'" (qtd. in Teitelboim 40).

48. "El asunto la apasionó siempre, hasta los límites de la obsesión, porque, en el fondo, cuando lo tocaba se estaba tocando a sí misma" (37).

49. "La dominaba una memoria tenaz, a prueba de tiempo, imborrable para el escarnio y el desprecio. Vivió poseída por aversiones sin remisión y por tabúes perpétuos" (37).

50. Mistral's failed relationships with men are, in turn, disturbingly linked to his assertion that she shunned physical relationships with men as the result of having been raped as a child: "¿De dónde nace el horror al contacto carnal? Ella lo ocultó como el secreto de sus secretos, bajo siete cerrojos, y la marcó para siempre. No obstante, en esa guerra de amor y miedo que fue su relación con Manuel, ante el reclamo, la presión y el atónito desconcierto del hombre que no entiende por qué se niega a consumar la relación amorosa, ella desliza una alusión que es como un orificio en el muro, para mirar al otro lado del secreto inconfesable . . . le confiesa que arrastra desde su niñez cierto trauma producido por un hecho brutal. Un mocetón que iba a su casa la violó cuando ella tenía siete años" (143).

51. See Molloy's "Female Textual Identities" for a discussion of this ongoing silence.

52. "¿Lo hizo para crear o para afirmar el mito romántico de la mujer de un solo amor? . . . Honradamente tengo que decir que no sé por qué lo hizo. Me digo, para entender, que tal vez ella quiso mezclar a los diversos hombres a los que amó porque en ellos buscaba a uno que no encontró" ("Introducción" xxii).

53. "'Autoretratos' [*sic*] en los que la verdadera Gabriela, la Gabriela de carne y hueso, asoma la cara—su cara de niña, su cara de joven, su cara de mujer—en su poesía" (xxxiii).

54. "Una en mí maté: / yo no la amaba" (183).

55. "Piedra y cielo tenía / a pies y a espaldas / y no bajaba nunca / a buscar 'ojos de agua'. // Donde hacía su siesta, / las hierbas se enroscaban / de aliento de su boca / y brasa de su cara" (183).

56. "Doblarse no sabía / la planta de montaña; / y al costado de ella, / yo me doblaba . . . // La dejé que muriese, / robándole mi entraña. / Se acabó como el águila / que no es alimentada" (183).

57. "—Buscad por las quebradas / y haced con las arcillas / otra águila abrasada. // Si no podéis, entonces, / ¡ay!, olvidadla. / Yo la maté. ¡Vosotras / también matadla!" (183).

58. See Olea for an analysis of "La otra" that reads the female voice killed in the poem as the other who is rejected by the dominant social order (158).

59. "Denme ahora las palabras / que no me dio la nodriza. / Las balbucearé demente / de la sílaba a la sílaba: / palabra 'expolio', palabra 'nada' / y palabra 'postrimería', / ¡aunque se tuerzan en mi boca / como las víboras mordidas!"

60. Estoy quemando lo que tuvimos:
       los anchos muros, las altas vigas,
       descuajando una por una
       las doce puertas que abrías
       y cegando a golpes de hacha
       el aljibe de la alegría
            Voy a esparcir, voleada,
       la cosecha ayer cogida,
       a vaciar odres de vino
       y a soltar aves cautivas;
       a romper como mi cuerpo
       los miembros de la 'masía'
       y a medir con brazos altos
       la parva de las cenizas. (184)

WORKS CITED

Aira, César. "Victoria Ocampo y la cultura Argentina: el triunfo de la perversión." *El Porteño* Febrero 1987: 64–66.

Almeida, José Maurício Gomes de. *A tradição regionalista no romance brasileiro (1857–1945)*. Rio: Achiamé, 1980.

Anderson, Benedict. *Imagined Communities: Reflections on the Origin and Spread of Nationalism*. New York: Verso, 1983.

Anderson Imbert, Enrique. *La crítica literaria contemporánea*. Buenos Aires: Ediciones Gure, 1957.

Baddeley, Oriana, and Valerie Fraser. *Drawing the Line: Art and Cultural Identity in Contemporary Latin America*. New York: Verso, 1992.

Baralis, Marta. "Necesidad de estudiar y valorar la prosa de Gabriela Mistral." *Filología* 12 (1966–1967): 193–201.

Barrios de Chungara, Domitila. *Let me speak! Testimony of Domitila, a Woman of the Bolivian Mines*. Trans. Victoria Ortiz. New York: Monthly Review Press, 1978.

Bastos, María Luisa. *Borges ante la crítica literaria argentina: 1923–1960*. Buenos Aires: Hispamérica, 1974.

Beer, Gabriella de. "Pedagogía y feminismo en una olvidada obra de Gabriela Mistral, 'Lecturas para mujeres'." *Monographic Review/Revista Monográfica* vi (1990): 211–220.

Bello, Andrés. "Autonomía cultural de América." *Conciencia intelectual de América: Antología del ensayo hispanoamericano (1836–1959)*. Ed. Carlos Ripoll. New York: Las Americas, 1966. 44–50.

Bergmann, Emilie, and Paul Julian Smith, eds. *¿Entiendes?: Queer Readings, Hispanic Writings*. Durham: Duke University Press, 1995.

Bosi, Alfredo. *História concisa da literatura brasileira*. São Paulo: Cultrix, 1983.

Butler, Judith. *Gender Trouble: Feminism and the Subversion of Identity*. New York: Routledge, 1990.

Cândido, Antônio. *Formação da literatura brasileira: momentos decisivos*. 6th ed. Belo Horizonte: Itatiaia, 1981.

Carlson, Marifran. *¡Feminismo!: The Woman's Movement in Argentina from its Beginnings to Eva Perón*. Chicago: Academy Chicago Publishers, 1988.

Castillo, Debra. *Talking Back: Toward a Latin American Feminist Literary Criticism*. Ithaca: Cornell University Press, 1992.

Concha, Jaime. *Gabriela Mistral*. Madrid: Ediciones Júcar, 1987.

Degler, Carl N. *In Search of Human Nature: The Decline and Revival of Darwinism in American Social Thought*. New York: Oxford University Press, 1991.

————. *Neither Black nor White: Slavery and Race Relations in Brazil and the United States*. Madison: University of Wisconsin Press, 1986.

Escudero, Alfonso, ed. *Recados: contando a Chile*. By Gabriela Mistral. Santiago de Chile: Editorial del Pacífico, 1957.

Figueira, Gastón. "Páginas desconocidas u olvidadas de Gabriela Mistral." *Inter-American Review of Bibliography* 20.2: 139–156.

Fiol-Matta, Licia. "The 'Schoolteacher of America': Gender, Sexuality, and Nation in Gabriela Mistral." *¿Entiendes?: Queer Readings, Hispanic Writings*. Ed. Emilie L. Bergmann and Paul Julian Smith. Durham: Duke University Press, 1995. 201–229.

Fiske, John. *Power Plays, Power Works*. New York: Verso, 1993.

Floresta, Nísia. *Opúsculo humanitário*. São Paulo: Cultrix, 1989.

Foster, David F. "Collected Essays of Literary Criticism." *Argentine Literature: A Research Guide*. 2nd ed. New York: Garland, 1982. 20–27.

————. *Gay and Lesbian Themes in Latin American Writing*. Austin: University of Texas Press, 1991.

————. *Sexual Textualities: Essays on Queer/ing Latin American Writing*. Austin: University of Texas Press, 1997.

Foucault, Michel. "What Is an Author?" *The Foucault Reader*. Ed. David Rabinow. New York: Pantheon, 1984. 101–120.

Franco, Jean. "Beyond Ethnocentrism: Gender, Power, and the Third-World Intelligentsia." *Marxism and the Interpretation of Culture*. Ed. Cary Nelson and Lawrence Grossberg. Chicago: University of Illinois Press, 1988. 503–515.

————. "Loca y no loca. La cultura popular en la obra de Gabriela Mistral." *Re-leer hoy a Gabriela Mistral: mujer, historia y sociedad en América Latina*. Ed. Gastón Lillo and J. Guillermo Renart. Ottawa: University of Ottawa Press, 1997. 27–42.

————. *Plotting Women: Gender and Representation in Mexico*. New York: Columbia University Press, 1989.

Freyre, Gilberto. *Casa grande e senzala*. Rio: José Olympio, 1943.

————. *O mundo que o português criou*. Rio: José Olympio, 1940.

————. *Sobrados e mucambos*. Rio: José Olympio, 1961.

Galvão, Patricia (Mara Lobo). *Parque Industrial: Romance Proletário*. São Paulo: Self-published, 1933.

————. *Parque Industrial: Romance Proletário*. São Paulo: Editora Alternativa, 1981.

Garrels, Elizabeth. "Piedra Azul, or the Colonial Paradise of Women." *Mama Blanca's Memoirs*. By Teresa de la Parra. Trans. Harriet de Onís and revised by

Frederick H. Fornoff. Ed. Doris Sommer. Pittsburgh: University of Pittsburgh Press, 1993. 136–150.

Gazarian-Gautier, Marie-Lise. "La prosa de Gabriela Mistral, o una verdadera joya desconocida." *Revista chilena de literatura* 36 (1990): 17–27.

Gilbert, Sandra M., and Susan Gubar. *The Madwoman in the Attic: The Woman Writer and the Nineteenth-Century Literary Imagination.* New Haven: Yale University Press, 1979.

Giusti, Roberto F. *Literatura y vida.* Buenos Aires: Nosotros, 1939.

———. *Visto y vivido: anécdotas, semblanzas, confesiones y batallas.* Buenos Aires: Losada, 1965.

Gomes, Ângela Maria de Castro. "A construção do homem novo: o trabalhador brasileiro." *Estado Novo: ideologia e poder.* Ed. Lúcia Lippi Oliveira, Mônica Pimenta Velloso, and Ângela Maria de Castro Gomes. Rio: Zahar, 1982. 151–166.

Gómez de Avellaneda, Gertrudis. "Women." Trans. Nina M. Scott. *Rereading the Spanish American Essay: Translations of 19th- and 20th-Century Women's Essays.* Ed. Doris Meyer. Austin: University of Texas Press, 1996. 25–39.

González Peña, Carlos. *Historia de la literatura mexicana desde los orígenes hasta nuestros dias.* México: Casa Editorial Cultura, 1928.

Greenberg, Janet Beth. "The Divided Self: Forms of Autobiography in the Writings of Victoria Ocampo." Diss. University of California, Berkeley, 1986.

———. "A Question of Blood: the Conflict of Sex and Class in the *Autobiografía* of Victoria Ocampo." *Women, Culture, and Politics in Latin America/Seminar on Feminism and Culture in Latin America.* Berkeley: University of California, 1990. 130–150.

Hahner, June E. *Emancipating the Female Sex: The Struggle for Women's Rights in Brazil, 1850–1940.* Durham: Duke University Press, 1990.

Heilbrun, Carolyn G. "Non-Autobiographies of 'Privileged' Women: England and America." *Life/Lines: Theorizing Women's Autobiography.* Ed. Bella Brodzki and Celeste Schenck. Ithaca: Cornell University Press, 1988. 62–76.

Henríquez Ureña, Pedro. *Literary Currents in Hispanic America.* Cambridge: Harvard University Press, 1946.

Hollanda, Heloísa Buarque de. "A roupa da Rachel: um estudo sem importância." *Estudos feministas* 0 (1992): 74–96.

Horan, Elizabeth Rosa. *Gabriela Mistral: An Artist and Her People.* Washington, D.C.: Organization of American States, 1994.

———. "Matrilineage, Matrilanguage: Gabriela Mistral's Intimate Audience of Women." *Revista Canadiense de Estudios Hispánicos* 14.3 (1990): 447–457.

Hurtado, Aída. *The Color of Privilege: Three Blasphemies on Race and Feminism.* Ann Arbor: University of Michigan Press, 1996.

Jiménez, Onilda A. *La crítica literaria en la obra de Gabriela Mistral.* Miami: Ediciones Universal, 1982.

King, John. *Sur: A Study of the Argentine Literary Journal and Its Role in the Development of a Culture, 1931–1970.* Cambridge: Cambridge University Press, 1986.

Kirchhoff, Frederick. *John Ruskin.* Boston: Twayne, 1984.

Lavrin, Asunción. *Women, Feminism, and Social Change in Argentina, Chile, and Uruguay, 1890–1940*. Lincoln: University of Nebraska Press, 1995.

Letona, René. "La prosa de Gabriela Mistral." *Cuadernos Hispanoamericanos* 472 (1989): 85–92.

Linhares, Temósticles. *História crítica do romance brasileiro (1728–1981)*. Belo Horizonte: Itatiaia, 1987.

Lisi, Cristina. "El proyecto cultural de la revista *Sur* (1931–1970). Un ejemplo de literatura 'marginal' en el rio de la plata." *La literatura en la sociedad de América Latina: Homenaje a Alejandro Losada*. Ed. José Morales Saraiva. Lima: Latinoamericana, 1987. 65–84.

Ludmer, Josefina. "Tretas del débil." *La sartén por el mango: encuentro de escritoras latinoamericanas*. Ed. Patricia Elena González and Eliana Ortega. Río Piedras, Puerto Rico: Ediciones Huracán, 1985. 47–54.

Martí, José. "Emerson." *Obras Completas*. Vol. 2. Caracas: n.p., 1964. 3–14.

Martins, Wilson. *A crítica literária no Brasil*. 1952. Rio: Francisco Alves, 1983.

Masiello, Francine. "Between Civilization and Barbarism: Women, Family and Literary Culture in Mid-Nineteenth-Century Argentina." *Cultural and Historical Grounding for Hispanic and Luso-Brazilian Feminist Literary Criticism*. Ed. Hernán Vidal. Minneapolis: Institute for the Study of Ideologies and Literature, 1989. 517–566.

———. *Between Civilization and Barbarism: Women, Nation, and Literary Culture in Modern Argentina*. Lincoln: University of Nebraska Press, 1992.

———. "Women, State, and Family in Latin American Literature of the 1920s." *Women, Culture and Politics in Latin America*. Berkeley: University of California Press, 1990. 27–47.

McNeillie, Andrew. Introduction. *The Common Reader, The First Series*. By Virginia Woolf. 1925. New York: Harcourt, 1983. ix-xv.

Menchú, Rigoberta. *Crossing Borders*. London: Verso, 1998.

———. *I, Rigoberta Menchú, an Indian Woman in Guatemala*. London: Verso, 1984.

Meyer, Doris. *Rereading the Spanish American Essay: Translations of 19th- and 20th-Century Women's Essays*. Austin: University of Texas Press, 1995.

Meyer, Michael C., and William L. Sherman. *The Course of Mexican History*. 2nd ed. New York: Oxford University Press, 1983.

Miguel Pereira, Lúcia. *Amanhecer*. Rio: José Olympio, 1938.

———. *Cabra-cega*. Rio: José Olympio, 1954.

———. *Em surdina*. Rio: Ariel, n.d. [1933].

———. *História da literatura brasileira: Prosa de ficção: de 1870 a 1920*. 4th ed. São Paulo: Editora da Universidade de São Paulo, 1988.

———. *A leitora e seus personagens: seleta de textos publicados em periódicos (1931–1943), e em livros*. Ed. Luciana Viégas. Rio: Graphia Editorial, 1992.

———. *Machado de Assis: estudo crítico e biográfico*. 6th ed. São Paulo: Editora da Universidade de São Paulo, 1988.

————. *Maria Luiza*. Rio: Schmidt, 1933.

————. *A vida de Gonçalves Dias*. Rio: José Olympio, 1943.

Miller, Francesca. "Latin American Feminism and the Transnational Arena." *Women, Culture and Politics in Latin America*. Berkeley: University of California Press, 1990. 10–26.

————. *Latin American Women and the Search for Social Justice*. Hanover: University Press of New England, 1991.

Miller, Nancy K. *Getting Personal: Feminist Occasions and Other Autobiographical Acts*. New York: Routledge, 1991.

Mistral, Gabriela. *Croquis Mexicanos*. Ed. Alfonso Calderón. Santiago de Chile: Editorial Nascimento, 1979.

————. *Desolación—Ternura—Tala—Lagar*. 4th ed. México: Porrúa, 1986.

————. "Electra in the Mist." Trans. Sylvia Molloy. *Women's Writing in Latin America: An Anthology*. Ed. Sara Castro-Klaren, Sylvia Molloy, and Beatriz Sarlo. Boulder, Colo.: Westview Press, 1991. 133–136.

————. *Lecturas para mujeres*. 1923. México: Porrúa, 1988.

————. *Poema de Chile*. Ed. Doris Dana. Santiago de Chile: Pomaire, 1967.

Moi, Toril. *Sexual/Textual Politics*. New York: Methuen, 1985.

Molloy, Sylvia. *At Face Value: Autobiographical Writing in Spanish America*. New York: Cambridge University Press, 1991.

————. "Dos proyectos de vida: *Cuadernos de infancia* de Norah Lange y *El archipiélago* de Victoria Ocampo." *Filología* (Buenos Aires) 20, 2 (1985): 279–293.

————. "Introduction to Part 2: Female Textual Identities: The Strategies of Self-Figuration." *Women's Writing in Latin America: An Anthology*. Ed. Sara Castro-Klaren, Sylvia Molloy, and Beatriz Sarlo. Boulder, Colo.: Westview Press, 1991. 107–124.

————. Review of *Sur: A Study of the Argentine Literary Journal and Its Role in the Literary Development of a Culture, 1931–1970*, by John King. *Bulletin of Hispanic Studies* 66 (1989): 108.

Molloy, Sylvia, and Robert McKee Irwin, eds. *Hispanisms and Homosexualities*. Durham: Duke University Press, 1998.

Monegal, Emir Rodríguez, et al. "Victoria Ocampo." *Vuelta* (México) 3: 30 (May 1979) 44–47.

Muschietti, Delfina. "Las mujeres que escriben: aquel reino anhelado del amor." *Nuevo texto crítico* 4 (1989): 79–102.

Neruda, Pablo. *Pablo Neruda: The Early Poems*. Trans. David Ossman and Carlos G. Hagen. New York: New Rivers Press, 1969.

Nicolau, Palma Guillén de. "Gabriela Mistral (1922–1924)" [Preface]. *Lecturas para mujeres*. 7th ed. By Gabriela Mistral. México: Porrúa, 1988.

————. "Introducción." *Desolación—Ternura—Tala—Lagar*. 4th ed. By Gabriela Mistral. México: Porrúa, 1986.

Ocampo, Victoria. *Autobiografía 2: El imperio insular*. Buenos Aires: Sur, 1980.

————. *Autobiografia 3: La rama de Salzburgo*. Buenos Aires: Sur, 1981.

————. "Correspondencia: Carta a Ernesto Sábato." *Sur* 211–212 (1952): 166–169.

————. "Correspondencia." *Sur* 213–214 (1952): 161–164.

————. *De Francesca a Beatrice*. Madrid: Revista de Ocidente, 1924.

————. *Soledad Sonora [Testimonios 4]*. Buenos Aires: Sudamericana, 1950.

————. *Testimonios* 1. Madrid: Revista de Ocidente, 1935.

————. *Testimonios* 2. Buenos Aires: Sur, 1941.

————. *Testimonios* 3. Buenos Aires: Sudamericana, 1946.

————. *Testimonios* 5. Buenos Aires: Sur, 1957.

————. *Testimonios* 6. Buenos Aires: Sur, 1963.

————. *Testimonios* 7. Buenos Aires: Sur, 1967.

————. *Testimonios* 8. Buenos Aires: Sur, 1971.

————. *Testimonios* 9. Buenos Aires: Sur, 1975.

————. *Testimonios* 10. Buenos Aires: Sur, 1977.

————. *33871 T. E.* (Lawrence of Arabia). Trans. David Garnett. New York: Dutton, 1963.

Ochoa P., and M. Alejandra. "Poética explícita de los escritos en prosa de Gabriela Mistral." *Acta Literaria* 14 (1989): 143–152.

Ohmann, Carol. "Emily Brontë in the Hands of Male Critics." *College English* 32.8 (May 1971): 906–913.

Olea, Raquel. "Otra lectura de 'La otra'." *Una palabra cómplice. Encuentro con Gabriela Mistral*. Santiago de Chile: Editorial Cuarto Proprio, 1997. 153–160.

O'Malley, Ilene V. *The Myth of the Revolution: Hero Cults and the Institutionalization of the Mexican State, 1920–1940*. New York: Greenwood Press, 1986.

Ortega y Gasset, José. Epílogo. *De Francesca a Beatrice*. By Victoria Ocampo. Madrid: Revista de Ocidente, 1924. 123–173.

Ortiz, Renato. *Cultura brasileira e identidade nacional*. São Paulo: Brasiliense, 1985.

Parra, Teresa de la. *Las memorias de Mamá Blanca*. Nanterre, France: ALLCA XX, 1988.

————. *Obra: Narrativa-Ensayos-Cartas*. Caracas: Biblioteca Ayacucho, 1982.

Peixoto, Afrânio. *Noções da história da literatura brasileira*. Rio: Francisco Alves, 1931.

Peña, Carlos González. *Historia de la literatura mexicana desde los orígenes hasta nuestros dias*. México: Casa Editorial Cultura, 1928.

Pinto, Cristina Ferreira. *O bildungsroman feminino: quatro exemplos brasileiros*. São Paulo: Perspectiva, 1990.

Pizarro, Ana. "Mistral, ¿Qué modernidad?" *Re-leer hoy a Gabriela Mistral: mujer, historia y sociedad en América Latina*. Ed. Gastón Lillo and J. Guillermo Renart. Ottawa: University of Ottawa Press, 1997. 43–52.

Pratt, Mary Louise. "Women, Literature, and National Brotherhood." *Women Culture and Politics in Latin America*. Berkeley: University of California Press, 1990. 48–73.

Queiroz, Rachel de. *O quinze*. São Paulo: Companhia Editora Nacional, 1930.

————. *O quinze*. 62nd ed. São Paulo: Editora Siciliano, 1997.

Rojas, Lourdes, and Nancy Saporta Sternbach. "Latin American Women Essayists: 'Intruders and Usurpers'." *The Politics of the Essay*. Ed. Ruth-Ellen Boetcher Joeres and Elizabeth Mittman. Bloomington: Indiana University Press, 1993. 172–195.

Rojas, Ricardo. *Historia de la literatura argentina*. Buenos Aires: Editorial Guillermo Kraft Limitada, 1960.

Rosowski, Susan J. "The Novel of Awakening." *The Voyage In: Fictions of Female Development*. Ed. Elizabeth Abel, Marianne Hirsch, and Elizabeth Langland. Hanover: University Press of New England, 1983. 49–68.

Ruskin, John. *Sesame and Lilies*. New York: John Wiley & Sons, 1889.

Sábato, Ernesto. "Correspondencia: 'Sobre la metafísica del sexo'." *Sur* 213–214 (1952): 158–161.

———. "Sobre la metafísica del sexo." *Sur* 209–210 (1952): 24–47.

Sandoval, Chela. "U.S. Third World Feminism: The Theory and Method of Oppositional Conciousness in the Postmodern World." *Genders* 10 (1991): 1–24.

Sandoval Sánchez, Alberto. "Hacía una lectura del cuerpo de mujer." *Ediciones de las mujeres (Isis Internacional)* 12 (1989): 47–57.

Sarlo, Beatriz. "Introduction to Part 3: Women, History, and Ideology." *Women's Writing in Latin America*. Ed. Sara Castro-Klarén, Sylvia Molloy, and Beatriz Sarlo. Boulder, Colo.: Westview Press, 1991. 231–248.

———. *La máquina cultural: maestras, traductores y vanguardistas*. Buenos Aires: Editorial Planeta Argentina, 1998.

———. *Una modernidad periférica: Buenos Aires, 1920 y 1930*. Buenos Aires: Ediciones Nueva Visión, 1988.

Sarmiento, Domingo Faustino. *Recuerdos de provincia*. Buenos Aires: Biblioteca Argentina, 1927.

Scarpa, Roque Esteban, ed. *Gabriela anda por el mundo*. By Gabriela Mistral. Santiago de Chile: Editorial Andrés Bello, 1978.

———, ed. *Gabriela piensa en . . . .* By Gabriela Mistral. Santiago de Chile: Editorial Andrés Bello, 1978.

Seminar on Women and Culture in Latin America. "Toward a History of Women's Periodicals in Latin America." *Women, Culture, and Politics in Latin America*. University of California Press, 1990.

Sharpe, Peggy. "Nísia Floresta: *Woman*." *Brasil/Brazil* 14 (1995): 83–120.

Sharpe-Valadares, Peggy. "Brazilian Women and Social Reform in Nísia Floresta's *Opúsculo*." *Brasil/Brazil* 1 (1988): 18–29.

Skidmore, Thomas E. "Racial Ideas and Social Policy in Brazil, 1870–1940." *The Idea of Race in Latin America, 1870–1940*. Ed. Richard Graham. Austin: University of Texas Press, 1990.

Sommer, Doris. *Foundational Fictions: The National Romances of Latin America*. Berkeley: University of California Press, 1991.

Spivak, Gayatri Chakravorty. "Three Women's Texts and a Critique of Imperialism." *"Race," Writing, and Difference*. Ed. Henry Louis Gates, Jr. Chicago: University of Chicago Press, 1986. 262–280.

Teitelboim, Volodia. *Gabriela Mistral pública y secreta: Truenos y silencios en la vida del primer Nobel latinoamericano.* Santiago de Chile: Ediciones BAT, 1991.

Telles, Norma. "Escritoras, escritas, escrituras." *História das mulheres no Brasil.* Org. Mary del Priore. São Paulo: Contexto, 1997. 401–442.

Vasconcelos, José. *Ulises criollo: La vida del autor escrita por él mismo.* México: Ediciones Botas, 1937.

Vaughan, Mary Kay. *The State, Education, and Social Class in Mexico 1880–1928.* DeKalb: Northern Illinois University Press, 1982.

Vázquez, Margot Arce de. *Gabriela Mistral: The Poet and Her Work.* Trans. Helene Masslo Anderson. New York: New York University Press, 1964.

Veríssimo, Érico. *O tempo e o vento.* Rio: Editora Globo, 1961–1963.

Woolf, Virginia. *The Common Reader, The First Series.* 1925. New York: Harcourt, 1983.

INDEX

Abortion, 27

A crítica literária no Brasil (Martins), 14, 16, 19

Aguirre la Cerda, Pedro, 100

"A la mujer mexicana" (Mistral), 97–99

A leitora e seus personagens: seleta de textos publicados emperiódicos (Miguel Pereira), 18

Alfaro Siqueiros, David, 84

"Alfonsina Storni" (Giusti), 57

"Al margen de Ruskin: algunas reflexiones sobre la lectura" (Ocampo), 80

Almeida, José Maurício Gomes de, 27

Amado, Jorge, 27, 28

Amanhecer (Miguel Pereira), 20, 23–25

Anderson, Benedict, 87

Anderson Imbert, Enrique, 16–17

Aranha, Graça, 41

Arce de Vázquez, Margot, 99–101, 102

Argentina, 11; education in, 3; national literature in, 14; Ocampo's relationship with, 48–49; women writers in, 4

Argentine Literature: A Research Guide (Foster), 56

"A roupa da Rachel: un estudo sem importância" (Buarque de Hollanda), 29

Assis, Machado de, 18, 31–33, 34, 35–38, 41, 43

Asúnsolo, Ignacio, 88

At Face Value (Molloy), 53

Augustini, Delmira, 15

Austen, Jane, 77

Author function, 8

Autobiographical form. See Personal/ autobiographical writing

Autobiographies, 8

"Autonomía cultural de America" (Bello), 7

A vida de Gonçalves Dias (Miguel Pereira), 32–40

Baddeley, Oriana, 84

Barrenechea, Ana María, 17

Barreto, Lima, 31, 32–33, 35, 38, 39

Barrios de Chungara, Domitila, 10

Bastos, Maria Luisa, 70

Bello, Andrés, 7

Bergamín, José, 59–61

Bergmann, Emilie, 13, 27

"Beyond Ethnocentrism: Gender, Power, and the Third-World Intelligentsia" (Franco), 7

Biographies, 8

Bloom, Harold, 65

Boas, Franz, 40, 42

Boedo-Florida polemic, 70

Bombal, María Luisa, 11, 106

Borges, Jorge Luis, 70, 74

Bosi, Alfredo, 19

Brazil, 11; education in, 3; impressionistic criticism in, 14; marriage in, 22; women writers in, 4
Brontë, Branwell, 77
Brontë, Charlotte, 77
Brontë, Emily, 69, 76–79
Browning, Elizabeth Barrett, 71
Brunet, Marta, 2
Bullrich, Eduardo, 70
Bunge, Delfina, 51
Burgos Debray, Elisabeth, 11
Butler, Judith, 6

Cabra-cega (Miguel Pereira), 20, 25–27
Canaã (Aranha), 41
Cândido, Antônio, 19
Caraffa, Brandán, 54
Carlson, Marifran, 58
"Carta a Virginia Woolf" (Ocampo), 67, 68
Casa grande e senzala (Freyre), 40–42
Castillo, Debra, 11–13
Children's rights, 98
Chile, 11; education in, 3; Mistral's relationship with, 100, 101
Ciclo da cana de açucar, 27, 28
Ciclo do cacau, 28
Civil Code, 22, 59
Class: Miguel Pereira on, 19, 33, 34, 35; Ocampo on, 49–50
Colette, 71–72, 78
Color of Privilege, The: Three Blasphemies on Race and Feminism (Hurtado), 9–10
Common Reader, A (Woolf), 72–73
Confederación Regional Obrera Mexicana, 85
"Contestación a un epílogo de Ortega y Gasset" (Ocampo), 55
Crepusculario (Neruda), 94
"Croquis Mexicanos" (Mistral), 96
Crossing Borders (Menchú), 10–11

Daireaux, Max, 52
Dante, 53, 55
Darío, Rubén, 101
De Francesca a Beatrice (Ocampo), 53–55, 56, 57
Degler, Carl, 42

Desolación (Mistral), 100, 101, 103–4
Desolación—Ternura—Tala—Lagar (Mistral), 103
"Dette à la France" (Ocampo), 68
Dias, Gonçalves, 18, 31, 32–40, 41, 43–44
Días Parrado, Flora, 2
"Divided Self, The" (Greenberg), 79
Divine Comedy, The (Dante), 53, 54
Doña Bárbara (Gallegos), 97
D'Ors, Eugenio, 95

Education, 3–4; Miguel Pereira on, 20, 26; Mistral on, 81, 82–85, 89, 91–94, 95, 98; Ocampo on, 51, 52, 89
"El desdén del oficio" (D'Ors), 95
"Electra en la niebla"/"Electra in the Mist" (Mistral), 82, 104–5
Eliot, T. S., 73
Elitism, 49–50, 52
Emerson, Ralph Waldo, 17
"Emily Brontë (Terra incognita)" (Ocampo), 68, 76–79
Em surdina (Miguel Pereira), 20, 21–23
¿Entiendes?: Queer Readings, Hispanic Writings (Bergmann and Smith), 27
Escritos de maturidade: seleta de textos publicados em periódicos (Miguel Pereira), 18
Escuelas hogar, 85, 88
Espirit (magazine), 60
Estado Novo, 41
Estrada, Angel de, 54
Eugenia, María, 15
European influence: Miguel Pereira and, 42–43, 64, 108; Mistral and, 83–84, 89, 108; Ocampo and, 64, 68–69, 108

Feminism, 7, 9. See also Gender inequality; Gender roles; Women writers; Mistral and, 93; Ocampo and, 50, 57, 58–63, 74–75
¡Feminismo!: The Woman's Movement in Argentina from Its Beginnings to Eva Peron (Carlson), 58
Ferré, Rosario, 11
Ferreira, Vaz, 15
Fiol-Matta, Licia, 82

Fiske, John, 6
Floresta, Nísia, 3, 109n 1
Flush (Woolf), 71
Formação da literatura brasileira (Cândido), 19
Foster, David, 27
Foucault, Michel, 8
Franco, Jean, 7, 97, 106
Fraser, Valerie, 84
Freyre, Gilberto, 40–42

Gabriela Mistral: The Poet and Her Work (Arce de Vázquez), 99–101
"Gabriela Mistral (1922–1924)" (Guillén de Nicolau), 83–84
Gabriela Mistral pública y secreta (Teitelboim), 101–3
Gallegos, Rómulo, 97
Galvão, Patricia, 27
Garro, Elena, 11
Gaskell, Elizabeth, 77
Gay and Lesbian Themes in Latin American Writing (Foster), 27
Gender inequality, 19–28. See also Feminism; Women writers
Gender roles: Miguel Pereira and, 23–25; Mistral and, 85–87, 91
Gilbert, Sandra, 65
Girondo, Oliverio, 70
Giusti, Roberto E., 56–57
Glantz, Margo, 11
Gómez de Avellaneda, Gertrudis, 17
Greenberg, Janet, 13, 58, 59, 65, 79
Gross, John, 72–73
Groussac, Paul, 54, 79
Gubar, Susan, 65
Guillén de Nicolau, Palma, 83–84, 88, 103

Hahner, June, 22
Heilbrun, Carolyn, 50
Henríquez Ureña, Pedro, 2–3, 7, 9, 15–16, 17, 18
"Himno Matinal de la 'Escuela Gabriela Mistral' de México" (Mistral), 93–94
Hispanisms and Homosexualities (Molloy and Irvin), 27
História concisa da literatura brasileira (Bosi), 19

"Historia de mi amistad con los libros ingleses" (Ocampo), 68
Historical perspective: Miguel Pereira and, 27–28; Mistral and, 96, 97; Ocampo and, 57, 66–67
Hollanda, Heloísa Buarque de, 29
Horan, Elizabeth, 89
Hurtado, Aída, 9–10

I, Rigoberta Menchú, an Indian Woman in Guatemala (Menchú), 10–11
Ibarbourou, Juana de, 15
Illegitimacy, 98–99
Imagined Communities: Reflections on the Origin and Spread of Nationalism (Anderson), 87
"Imperfect Critics" (Eliot), 73
Impressionistic criticism, 14, 72–73
Intelligentsia, 7
Irwin, Robert McKee, 27

Jacobs, Barbara, 11
Jane Eyre (Brontë), 77
Juana Inés de la Cruz (Sor Juana), 13
Juárez, Benito, 3
Juston, Agustín P., 59

King, John, 58, 119n 43
Kirchhoff, Frederick, 81
Kirkpatrick, Gwen, 13

"La abandonada" (Mistral), 104, 105
"La ansiosa" (Mistral), 104
Lacau, María Hortensia, 17
La crítica literaria contemporánea (Anderson Imbert), 16–17
"La desasida" (Mistral), 104
"La desvelada" (Mistral), 104
"La fervorosa" (Mistral), 104
"La fugitiva" (Mistral), 104
Lagar (Mistral), 99
Lange, Norah, 70, 106
"La otra" (Mistral), 103, 104
"La que camina" (Mistral), 104
Las memorias de Mamá Blanca (Parra), 96–97
"La soldadera," 86–87

Latin American Women and the Search for Social Justice (Miller), 13, 58
"La vida privada" (Mounier), 60
Lavrin, Asunción, 58
Lawrence, T. E., 62
Lecturas para mujeres (Mistral), 81, 82, 83, 87–88, 89, 91, 92, 93, 95, 97–98, 104, 105, 106
Lematire, Jules, 14
Lesbianism: Miguel Pereira and, 27; Mistral and, 82, 102–3
Let Me Speak! Testimony of Domitila, a Woman of the Bolivian Mines (Barrios de Chungara), 10
Letona, René, 89
Lida de Malkiel, María Rosa, 17
"Lilies: of Queens' Gardens" (Ruskin), 81
Linhares, Temósticles, 27
Lisi, Cristina, 46, 58
Lispector, Clarice, 11, 21
Literary criticism, 8–9, 14–17; impressionistic, 14, 72–73; by Miguel Pereira, 18, 19, 29–45; by Mistral, 81, 105–6; by Ocampo, 47, 50, 56–58, 63–67, 70, 72–73
Literary Currents in Hispanic America (Henríquez Ureña), 2, 7, 15
Literatura y vida (Giusti), 57
"Locas mujeres" (Mistral), 103, 104
"Loca y no loca. La cultura popular en la obra de Gabriela Mistral" (Franco), 97
Lopes de Almeida, Júlia, 30–31
Lorde, Audre, 7

Machado de Assis: estudo crítico e biográfico (Miguel Pereira), 18, 31–32, 36, 39, 43
Madwoman in the Attic, The: The Woman Writer and the Nineteenth-Century Imagination (Gilbert and Gubar), 65
"Maestranzas de Noche" (Neruda), 94–95
"Malandanzas de una autodidacta" (Ocampo), 51
Mallea, Eduardo, 70
Malraux, André-Georges, 62
Marañon, Gregorio, 59
Maria Luiza (Miguel Pereira), 20–21
Marinetti, Filippo, 73, 74

Marriage: Miguel Pereira on, 21–23, 24; Mistral on, 102
Martí, José, 9, 17
Martins, Wilson, 14, 16, 19
Masiello, Francine, 5, 13, 49, 75, 106
Matto de Turner, Clorinda, 5
McNeillie, Andrew, 72–73
Meléndez, Concha, 17
Menchú, Rigoberta, 10–11
Menino de engenho (Lins do Rego), 27
Mexican Ministry of Education, 81, 82, 85
Mexican Revolution, 84, 85–87, 101
Mexico, 11; education in, 3; Mistral's relationship with, 82–88, 101; national literature in, 14; women writers in, 4
Miguel Pereira, Lúcia, 1–2, 15, 16, 18–45, 46; on class, 19, 33, 34, 35; on education, 20, 26; erasure of women's voices, 18, 44–45, 107; on gender inequality, 19–28; on gender roles, 23–25; literary criticism by, 18, 19, 29–45; on marriage, 21–23, 24; novels by, 19–28; on race, 19, 31–45; 18–19; women writers and, 5, 6, 19, 28–29, 30–31
Miller, Francesca, 13–14, 58, 85–86, 92–93
Mistral, Gabriela, 1, 2–3, 15, 80–106, 108; on children's rights, 98; on education, 81, 82–85, 89, 91–94, 95, 98; feminism and, 93; on gender roles, 85–87, 91; on illegitimacy, 98–99; industrialization and, 94–95; lesbianism of, 82, 102–3; literary criticism by, 81, 105–6; on marriage, 102; and motherhood theme, 3, 81–82, 86, 87, 90–92, 98–99, 100, 105; myths surrounding, 101–3; on nature, 96, 99; Nobel Prize won by, 69, 81, 101; Ocampo on, 56, 69; on race, 97; on teaching, 82, 92–93; women writers and, 5, 6
Mitre, Bartolomé, 7, 64
Mohanty, Chandra, 7
Moi, Toril, 66
Molloy, Sylvia, 5, 27, 47, 53, 82
Morello-Frosch, Marta, 13
Mothers/motherhood: Miguel Pereira on, 35–37; Mistral on, 3, 81–82, 86, 87, 90–92, 98–99, 100, 105

Mounier, Emmanuel, 60
Mrs. Dalloway (Woolf), 70–71
Mujer antigua (ancient woman), 90–91, 93, 95
Mujer nueva (new woman), 90
Muschietti, Delfina, 54
Mussolini, Benito, 100

Nationalist literature, 7–9, 14; Miguel
   Pereira and, 28, 29–31, 41–42; Mistral
   and, 88–89, 97–98
Nature, 96, 99
Neruda, Pablo, 94–95
Nervo, Amado, 100
Newman, Kathleen, 13
Noailles, Anna de, 55, 67, 75, 78
Normal schools (teacher education), 3–4

*O bildungsroman feminino: quatro
   exemplos brasileiros* (Pinto), 20
Objectivity, 48, 53
Obra: Narrativa-Ensayos-Cartas (de la
   Parra), 14
Obregón, Alvaro, 82, 85
Ocampo, Silvina, 11
Ocampo, Victoria, 1, 2, 11, 15, 16, 46–79;
   as an American, 49, 59, 64, 68–69; as an
   autodidact, 51; on class, 49–50; as a
   common reader, 73–74, 80–81; on
   education, 51, 52, 89; elitism attributed
   to, 49–50, 52; feminism and, 50, 57, 58–
   63, 74–75; French used by, 49, 52;
   literary criticism by, 47, 50, 56–58, 63–
   67, 70, 72–73; personal/autobiographical
   form of, 2, 46–49, 50–51, 53, 54, 56, 58,
   63–67, 107–8; as a translator, 52–53;
   women writers and, 5, 6, 47–49, 50, 55–
   56, 65–66, 67, 72, 75
Ohmann, Carol, 109–10n 8
O'Malley, Ilene, 86
O quinze (de Queiroz), 28–29, 29
Orlando (Woolf), 71–72, 74
Orozco, José, 84
Orpheé, Elvira, 11
Ortega y Gasset, José, 55–56, 58, 64, 66,
   73–74
Ortiz, Renato, 41–42, 45
O tempo e o vento (Veríssimo), 28

*Panorama de la Littérature Hispano-
   Américaine* (Daireaux), 52
Parque Industrial (Galvão), 27
Parra, Teresa de la, 14, 96–97, 98, 106
Patriarchy, 25, 26, 67, 101
"Perfect Critic, The" (Eliot), 73
Personal/autobiographical writing, 8, 9–
   11; Mistral and, 96–97; Ocampo and, 2,
   46–49, 50–51, 53, 54, 56, 58, 63–67,
   107–8
Pineda, Alberto, 102
Pinto, Cristina Ferreira, 20
Poema de Chile (Mistral), 96–97
Poniatowska, Elena, 11
Pratt, Mary Louise, 13, 87, 96
Prosa de ficção: de 1870 a 1920 (Miguel
   Pereira), 18, 30–31, 38, 39, 44
Proust, Marcel, 71, 75
Public schools, 3
Public versus private sphere. See Historical
   perspective; Nationalist literature;
   Personal/autobiographical writing;
   Regional literature
Puerto Rico, 11

Queiroz, Rachel de, 28–29

Rabutin-Chantal, Marie de, 55
Race: Miguel Pereira on, 19, 31–45; Mistral
   on, 97
"Racial Ideas and Social Policy in Brazil,
   1870–1940" (Skidmore), 40
"Racine et Mademoiselle" (Ocampo), 68
Ramos, Graciliano, 27, 28, 29
Recuerdos de provincia (Sarmiento), 8
Regional literature, 26–27, 28, 29
Rego, José Lins do, 27, 28
Revista de Occidente, 55
Rivera, Diego, 84
Rodríguez Monegal, Emir, 79
Rojas, Lourdes, 5
Romance nordestino, 26–27
Romero, Sílvio, 32, 40
Room of One's Own, A (Woolf), 67, 72,
   74, 75
Rosowski, Susan, 21
Ruskin, John, 80–81, 95

Sábato, Ernesto, 61–63, 64, 66
Sacred Wood, The (Eliot), 73
Sandoval, Chela, 7
Sandoval Sánchez, Alberto, 81
Sarlo, Beatriz, 52, 117n 19
Sarmiento, Domingo Faustino, 3, 8, 64, 83
"'Schoolteacher of America, The': Gender, Sexuality and Nation in Gabriela Mistral" (Fiol-Matta), 82
Seminar on Women and Culture in Latin America, 11, 13
"Sesame: Of Kings' Treasures" (Ruskin), 80, 81
Sesame and Lilies (Ruskin), 80, 95
Sexuality: Miguel Pereira on, 24–25; Mistral on, 82
Sexual Textualities: Essays on Queer/ing Latin American Writing (Foster), 27
Showalter, Elaine, 12
Sierra, Justo, 92
Skidmore, Thomas, 40
Smith, Paul Julian, 27
Sobrados e mucambos (Freyre), 40
"Sobre la metafísica del sexo" (Sábato), 61
Sommer, Doris, 7
"Sonetos de la muerte" (Mistral), 104
Speratti, Piñero, Emma Susana, 17
Storni, Alfonsina, 5, 15
Subjectivity, 48, 64
Sur (journal), 46, 57, 58, 59, 60, 61, 62, 63, 70
Sur: a study of the Argentine literary journal (King), 58

Tala (Mistral), 103
Talking Back: Toward a Latin American Feminist Literary Criticism (Castillo), 11–13
Teachers/teaching, 4, 82, 92–93
Teitelboim, Volodia, 101–3
Telles, Norma, 109n 1
Testimonios (Ocampo), 2, 48, 50, 56, 58, 63, 64–69, 72, 74, 79
Third World: feminist theory in, 9; intelligentsia of, 7
To the Lighthouse (Woolf), 72

Ulises criollo: La vida del autor escrita por él mismo, 8
Unión Argentina de Mujeres, 58–59
Ureta, Romelio, 101–102
Uruguay, 3

Vasconcelos, José, 8, 82–83, 85, 88, 92, 95, 101
Vega, Ann Lydia, 11
Veríssimo, Érico, 28
Veríssimo, José, 32, 40
"Viaje olvidado'" (Ocampo), 68
Victoria, Laura, 2
Victoria, Queen, 70, 75
Villa, Pancho, 85
"Virginia Woolf, Orlando y Cía" (Ocampo), 68, 69–76
Virginia Woolf en su diario (Ocampo), 74
Visto y vivido: anécdotas, semblanzas, confesiones y batallas (Giusti), 56–57
von Martius, C. F. P., 34, 35
von Spix, J. B., 34, 35
Voyage Out, The (Woolf), 70

Whitening ideal, 40, 41
Williams, Raymond, 6
Women, Culture, and Politics in Latin America (Bergmann), 11, 13
Women, Feminism, and Social Change in Argentina, Chile, and Uruguay (Lavrin), 58
"Women, Literature, and National Brotherhood" (Pratt), 96
Women of color, 9–10. See also Race
Women writers, 2–3, 4–9; Miguel Pereira and, 19, 28–29, 30–31; Mistral and, 5, 6; Ocampo and, 5, 6, 47–49, 50, 55–56, 65–66, 67, 72, 75
Woolf, Virginia, 55, 67–76, 77, 78
Work: Miguel Pereira on, 22, 25; Ocampo on, 51–52
Wuthering Heights (Brontë), 76–79

Years, The (Woolf), 72

Zapata, Emiliano, 86, 87